MORE ADVANCE PRAISE FOR

HARLEM NOCTURNE:

"A definitive and arresting account of three women artists. Farah Griffin gathers an array of Harlem stories and incorporates them into a wonderfully written and well-grounded narrative describing the artistic experiences and everyday lives of these three unique women. *Harlem Nocturne* is both intimate and comprehensive in its exploration of black women's creativity during World War II. A rich history that investigates the imagination and originality of black women's expressive culture in mid-20th century America, this book is timely and important."

—Deborah Willis, author of *Posing Beauty: African American Images from the 1890s to the Present*

"Farah Jasmine Griffin has written, beautifully and powerfully, about the complex intersection of gender, race, and place in the lives of three extraordinary black women. In her delicate hands, Pearl Primus, Ann Petry, and Mary Lou Williams stand as 'representative women,' exemplars of imagination at work and of the daunting task of the art of living in trying political times. As we get to know them, their lives narrate a distinctive story that offers us advice about how to live with courage, power, and beauty."

—Eddie S. Glaude, Jr., Princeton University, author of *In A Shade of Blue: Pragmatism and the Politics of Black America*

"Readers who accept Farah Jasmine Griffin's invitation to imagine Harlem in the 1940s through the eyes of three remarkable women— Pearl Primus, Ann Petry, and Mary Lou Williams—will be richly rewarded. Wearing her erudition lightly, Griffin brilliantly illuminates a place and time of enormous hope and achievement. *Harlem Nocturne* is an inspiring and inspired study of the artistic imagination in conversation with an American democracy tainted by injustice. It is, quite simply, a joy to read."

—Gayle Wald, author of *Shout, Sister, Shout!: The Untold Story of Rock-and-Roll Trailblazer Sister Rosetta Tharpe*

"As elegant and dynamic as the figures that it chronicles, *Harlem Nocturne* is a groundbreaking cultural history of three black women artists at work in 1940s New York City. Farah Jasmine Griffin is a dazzling storyteller whose lyrical prose evokes the musical cadences of a Toni Morrison novel. Her study beckons us to soar with dancer-choreographer Pearl Primus, to walk with novelist Ann Petry as she chronicles the streets of Harlem, and to roll with pioneering jazz musician and composer Mary Lou Williams as each woman made art that laid down the blueprint for the modern Civil Rights Movement. By placing their lives in conversation with one another, *Harlem Nocturne* illuminates the myriad ways that Primus, Petry and Williams helped to shape the social, political, and cultural landscape of their city. As much a love letter to New York as it is to the heroism of these artists, Griffin's study is a work of incandescent beauty."

—Daphne A. Brooks, Princeton University, author of *Bodies in Dissent: Spectacular Performances of Race and Freedom, 1850–1910*

"An engaging biography of three remarkable women who taught art to reflect life."

—*Kirkus Reviews*

HARLEM
Nocturne

HARLEM
Nocturne

WOMEN ARTISTS &
PROGRESSIVE
POLITICS DURING
WORLD WAR II

Farah Jasmine Griffin

BASIC *CIVITAS*
A MEMBER OF THE PERSEUS BOOKS GROUP
New York

Published by BasicCivitas Books,
A Member of the Perseus Books Group

Books published by Basic Books are available at special discounts for bulk purchases in the United States by corporations, institutions, and other organizations. For more information, please contact the Special Markets Department at the Perseus Books Group, 2300 Chestnut Street, Suite 200, Philadelphia, PA 19103, or call (800) 810-4145, ext. 5000, or e-mail special.markets@perseusbooks.com.

Typeset in 11.5-point Arno Pro by the Perseus Books Group

Library of Congress Cataloging-in-Publication Data

Griffin, Farah Jasmine.

Harlem nocturne : women artists and progressive politics during World War II / Farah Jasmine Griffin.—First [edition].

pages cm

Includes bibliographical references and index.

ISBN 978-0-465-01875-8 (hardback)—ISBN 978-0-465-06997-2 (e-book) (print) 1. African American women artists—New York (State)—New York—History—20th century. 2. African American women artist—Political activity—New York (State)—New York—History—20th century. 3. Petry, Ann, 1908–1997. 4. Primus, Pearl. 5. Williams, Mary Lou, 1910–1981. 6. New York (N.Y.)—Intellectual life—20th century. 7. Harlem (New York, N.Y.)—Intellectual life—20th century. I. Title.

NX512.3.A35G75 2013

704'.04208996073—dc23

2013010855

10 9 8 7 6 5 4 3 2 1

For My Mother,
Wilhelmena Griffin,
With Love and Gratitude

In America's bosom we have the roots of Democracy, but the roots do not mean there are leaves. The tree could easily grow bare. We will never relax our war effort abroad but we must fight at home with equal fierceness. This is an all out war; we will not stop fighting until everyone is free from inequality.

PEARL PRIMUS

There is a deep public reverence for—a love of—democracy in America and a deep democratic tradition. This love of democracy has been most powerfully expressed and pushed forward by our great public intellectuals and artists.

CORNEL WEST

Nations rely on artists and intellectuals to create images of, and to tell stories about, the national past. Competition for political leadership is in part a competition between differing stories about a nation's self-identity, and between differing symbols of its greatness.

RICHARD RORTY

CONTENTS

PROLOGUE

New York beckoned, and they came. One came as a child, brought by immigrant parents. The other two came as adult women seeking the freedom to create themselves and their art.

They were shaped by this city: their sense of the possible, the movement of their bodies, their style. They walked. They looked. They listened. They gave to the city. They danced for it, wrote it, set it to music. New York beckoned; they came.

New York told them anything was possible, told them there were no boundaries. There were. Though the city welcomed them as visitors, students, teachers, and entertainers, as residents they were not always received with enthusiasm. So at some point, they all lived in Harlem: the Black Mecca, born of the migration of black peoples from the Caribbean and the American South, the antiblack violence that erupted in other parts of the city, and the entrepreneurial energies of African American real-estate developer Philip A. Payton Jr. Harlem, race capital. Eventually, the immigrant's daughter moved to another historic black neighborhood—Bedford-Stuyvesant in Brooklyn.

Harlem: Who wanted to live anywhere else? If given the choice, they probably would have chosen Harlem, but they would have liked having the choice. So each, in her own way, protested the limitations placed on her life and her people, meanwhile helping to build a city within a city: a place full of black and brown faces speaking a multitude of languages, living high and living low, making love, making music, making word-worlds, making new peoples. It was a city of swinging rhythms and bebop changes; a city of weary brown-faced children and adults—some enraged, others resigned; a city that danced the Lindy Hop, modern choreography, and African isolations.

Certainly, these women were not Harlem's only architects; nor were they its best known. But they, like others, tried to leave their mark on New York. They built a city where people mattered. They were concerned about poor and working people, about women and children, about the disenfranchised and the dispossessed. They brought a radical vision from the 1930s into a new decade, helping to create a political culture that would inspire people worldwide. Thanks to their efforts and the efforts of others like them, Harlem, in the 1940s, sent the first black New Yorker to Congress; helped to elect an Italian Harlemite to that august body, too; and sent a member of the Communist Party to New York's City Council.

This energetic optimism was often tempered by the ongoing reality of American racial prejudice, even in New York. Following the bombing of Pearl Harbor in 1941, their city feared for itself. It experienced a patriotism so broad that even the mob offered its services. Their city saw its boys (and girls) enlist, and saw its patriotic black sons consigned to a segregated military and sent to the Jim Crow South for boot camp. Their neighborhood joined in the urban uprisings of 1943 that spread from Los Angeles and Texas to Detroit. After the riots, Harlem watched its middle class move to Queens and the Bronx and its white habitués abandon its nightlife. Both would have a devastating impact upon the neighborhood's economy.

Still, New York beckoned. It recognized their differences as a source of originality. *You should come,* the city told them; *you should be here, you belong, you are invited, you are welcome, stay a while. You are smart enough, beautiful enough, hip enough, tough enough, enterprising enough. You are mine.*

And—as with every heart that races at the speed of New York streets, every eye struck with awe at the grand façade of an elegant apartment building or the sheer audacity of a sky-scraper, every mouth that smiles at a brief encounter, an over-heard conversation, or the constant chatter—these women fell in love with this city. At times, they grew tired, a little weary, and sojourned away from the chaos and confusion of urban life. But always, they couldn't wait to return, to be back in the crowd, in the thick of it. New York beckoned, and, yes, they came, again and again. Amid the noise, the rush, the thrill, and the trepidation, they came, they settled, they made homes, and they made art.

There was also a cherished quiet. The still silence of a small apartment, where a woman sat at a typewriter in the hour just before dawn. A dance studio where a young woman marked her steps before her students or other members of the com-pany arrived. An early-morning walk through the northern tip of Central Park, where newly fallen snow muffled the sounds of the city and revealed a striking magenta hat. On a pink-covered twin bed in a Sugar Hill apartment, a woman tried to notate the sounds in her head so that she might eventually sleep in peace. These women were alone but not lonely. They knew solitude, welcomed it and the gifts it bore. They welcomed the rare chance to hear their own thoughts, before the city stirred, before rousing from that pink-covered bed.

Their city is a place that nurtures, produces, and challenges not only their art, but also their ideas, their thought, their aesthetic. In their city, they wear pompadours and platform shoes. One woman makes her clothes; one dresses like a bobby-soxer, complete with ankle socks and saddle shoes; and one is inclined to the fashionable life, with her Dior gowns, B. Altman shoes, furs, and orchid corsages. Platforms and pompadours sweep them up high, revealing foreheads and intelligent eyes. Not hiding behind bangs, they are forthright, honest—and the added height doesn't hurt. Platforms and pompadours "splendidly uprising toward clear skies."[1]

Their New York is Sugar Hill, Strivers Row, The Hollow, Upper East Side, The Village, and Bed-Stuy. Their New York speaks Spanish and Jive, French, and West Indian–inflected Queen's English, in dialects born of the Yankee North and the Black South. And some Saturday mornings the Italians, Puerto Ricans, West Indians, Jews, and southern migrants leave their own Harlem to mingle under the bridge on Park Avenue from 111th to 116th—the open-air markets beneath the railroad tracks. There, the writer tells us, the vendors "quarrel, bargain, exchange insults with customers in Spanish, Italian, Yiddish and American ranging from tough East Side, New York to the soft accents of the Old South." Under the bridge, "stalls piled with . . . a bewildering variety of foods . . . long-grain Carolina rice, Spanish saffron, chili powder, fresh ginger root, plantains, water cress, olive oil, olives, spaghetti and macaroni, garlic, basil, zucchini, finocchio, white corn meal, collards, mustard greens, black-eyed peas, big hominy and little hominy, spare-ribs, hot peppers, pimentos, coconuts, pineapples, mangoes."[2]

New York, in all of its delirious deliciousness, beckoned, and they came.

INTRODUCTION

N ew York is a city of culture and commerce, skyscrapers and bustling crowds, opportunity and deferred dreams. There are many ways to know this city, but being acquainted with its artists, especially if they are artists who are concerned with the complex lives of ordinary people, is particularly illuminating. Such artists help us understand New York's particularities while also giving voice and vision to universal feelings: fear and longing, trepidation and possibility. Through them we experience the city: navigate its crowds, walk its streets, and ride its subways. We see how they relate to those who share their environment and how they address—or ignore—the social and political concerns of the day. Attending to the artists and their work helps us to remember that people are always bigger than the theories, narratives, and histories that seek to explain, define, narrate, and contain them.

The generation of artists who lived and worked in New York, especially in Harlem, during and immediately following World War II understood that people could not be contained or fully explained by academic or political theories. The stories of three such artists drive the narrative of *Harlem Nocturne,* an exploration of politics and culture in New York during the 1940s: choreographer and dancer Pearl Primus, writer Ann Petry, and composer and pianist Mary Lou Williams. Although they are not well known to contemporary readers, Primus, Petry, and Williams were among the city's most celebrated artists in that decade. Each was inspired by her times to produce highly innovative art that communicated the aspirations of everyday people.

None of these women were native New Yorkers. Petry, a fourth-generation New Englander, was born in Old Saybrook, Connecticut, in 1908. Williams was born in Atlanta in 1910 and migrated with her family to Pittsburgh when she was a girl. Primus was born in Trinidad in 1919 and came with her family to New York when she was three years old. Primus spent her teenage years in Harlem. Petry arrived there as a newlywed in 1938. Williams settled in Harlem in 1943, after over a decade on the road.

Primus and Williams would become friends and collaborators while both were working at Café Society, the politically leftist jazz club that presented some of New York's most important and exciting talent. Surely Petry, the loner, was aware of them, but there is no evidence that she knew them personally. However, this is not a group biography. Primus, Petry, and Williams are bound together by a place and a time, and together they give us an understanding of the relationship between artistic endeavor and political aspiration. During the 1940s all three women were producing celebrated art, actively promoting progressive causes, and working to merge their political and aesthetic concerns. Each sought to expand the contours of the American ideal of democracy to include the most marginalized peoples. Each commented upon and critiqued the limited practice of American democracy. And each strove to contribute to American culture by bringing to it the perspective, history, and traditions of its citizens of African descent.

Importantly, all three women were recognized by their peers and by the arts establishment as significant artists. They also shared an extraordinary sense of themselves, a belief in their capacity and a willingness to build upon their natural talent through intense preparation, practice, and learning. In addition to being artists and activists, each was also an intellectual who critically engaged questions about her chosen art form.

The first half of the decade offered these women unprecedented opportunity. This would change by decade's end. By that time in each woman's experience, the range of opportunities was narrowing, the result of changing politics and shifting aesthetic sensibilities. By the early 1950s, Petry, Primus, and Williams had all left New York. Primus, who had been traveling in West Africa, returned to the United States to find herself under investigation by the FBI. Williams toured Europe and wouldn't return for two years; it would be decades before she reached heights similar to those of the earlier years. Petry spent the rest of her life in New England. Still, they all continued to be productive artists in spite of these changes.

Although *Harlem Nocturne* focuses on individual women, it also seeks to place them in the context of the city and the organizations and institutions that helped to shape them and their art. The war years offered a brief period of possibility and hope for many, especially for white women and black Americans of both genders. These years tested the capacity of the United States to live up to its democratic ideals. During this time, a new group of gutsy, confident, and insistent black people joined a generation of progressive whites who were committed to a vision of their nation as a place of potential, a place capable of change and worth fighting for. Many of this generation would later be challenged and silenced by Cold War politics, or would capitulate to those politics, but not before laying the groundwork for the militant activism that exploded in later decades. Tactics that we most often associate with the civil rights movement in the fifties and sixties—sit-ins, freedom rides, economic boycotts, and mass marches—originated in the forties. The first March on Washington was to have taken place in 1941, and the plans for it became the blueprint for the 1963 March on Washington for Jobs and Freedom.

The forties are a period of great importance in American history and culture. In popular history, it is the time of "the Greatest Generation"—those young men who served their country in the armed services and in so doing helped to free the world for democracy. But the idolization of these young men also highlighted a central contradiction: as the "Greatest Generation" was fighting for freedom abroad, women and African Americans were still lobbying for equality at home. So for American women, it was also the era of Rosie the Riveter and the emergence of the "woman's film," when women's narratives first hit the silver screen. For African Americans, it was the age of Double V—or Double Victory—where black Americans fought not only overseas for their country but also to be recognized as citizens at home (Victory at Home and Abroad). In American music, it was the time when the swing era gave way to bebop and rhythm and blues.

Throughout the 1940s, Primus, Petry, and Williams experienced a particularly fecund period of creativity, taking advantage of a brief era of openness and opportunity. Four factors contributed to creating the conditions for the social and artistic movement of which these women were a part: World War II, the Double V Campaign, the Second Great Migration of African Americans, and the Popular Front in politics, art, and culture that first coalesced during the Great Depression, but continued through the war years.

Because of the absence of men, many US women were afforded greater opportunity during the war years than they had seen in earlier times—or would see in the times immediately thereafter. This flowering of opportunity reached black women, too. Though most black women continued to work as domestic servants, some began to find work as clerks, nurses, teachers, and seamstresses. Those who entered the war industry were relegated to the most menial, labor-intensive tasks. A few black women in the skilled trades fought their way into newly integrated unions.

Petry, Primus, and Williams were profoundly influenced by the Double V Campaign. Through Double V, African Americans insisted upon their social and civil rights while at the same time committing themselves to the war effort. For black people, the war provided an opportunity to accelerate their demands for equality. As the nation fought a war against fascism, a war for democracy, it also sought to present itself as a land of equality and opportunity for all of its citizens. Black Americans highlighted the distance between this ideal of America and the reality of ongoing racial inequality, often through the black press and civil rights organizations.

The Double V Campaign was part of a larger social movement whose ultimate goal was the destruction of Jim Crow and the dismantling of the infamous 1896 *Plessy v. Ferguson* decision, which legalized and helped to institutionalize racial segregation in public accommodations. The movement focused on segregation in the armed services and reached its apex with the March on Washington movement in 1941, organized by civil rights leader A. Philip Randolph, founder of the Brotherhood of Sleeping Car Porters union, and political strategist and organizer Bayard Rustin. The march, which was planned in order to protest discrimination in the defense industries, had its beginnings in May of that year when Randolph issued a "Call to Negro America to March on Washington for Jobs and Equal Participation in National Defense" on July 1, 1941. Within a month it was estimated that 100,000 protesters would attend. President Franklin D. Roosevelt appealed to Randolph and Rustin to call the march off, hoping to avoid the embarrassment of a mass protest against racism in the midst of a war against Nazism. When they refused, he issued Executive Order 8802, establishing the President's Fair Employment Practices Committee, which barred discrimination in defense industries and federal bureaus. Only then did Randolph call off the proposed march. But even though the march never happened,

Randolph and Rustin's proposal marked the beginning of the modern civil rights movement, the long, slow road to *Brown v. Board of Education* and beyond. For while the Double V Campaign used the war to focus on the armed services, it also concerned itself with segregation and discrimination in housing and employment.

The political activism evident in the Double V Campaign was undergirded by the tremendous growth of black urban populations during the war years. Between 1916 and 1930, approximately 1.5 million African Americans moved to northern cities in response to the call for industrial laborers. The Second Great Migration was larger and more sustained than the first. Between 1940 and 1970, over 5 million black southerners migrated north and west. By the end of World War II, the majority of African Americans were urban, and they were transforming the face of American cities politically, economically, and culturally. The migrants were often the subjects of Primus's and Petry's art, and they provided a significant portion of Primus's and Williams's audiences. Each woman aligned her art with the aspirations of migrants: the desire for equal citizenship, for adequate housing, for access to educational and economic opportunity, and for freedom from racial violence and police brutality.

Finally, the political and aesthetic sensibilities of these women were encouraged by a number of left-leaning organizations and institutions. The Popular Front was a program initiated by the Communist Party in response to the economic crisis of the Great Depression and the rise of fascism. At its Seventh World Congress in 1935, the Comintern—the inter-

national association of Communist organizations created by
V. I. Lenin in 1917—replaced its call for a proletariat-led global
revolution with a call for a "broad People's Front" coalition of
liberals, radicals, trade unionists, farmers, socialists, blacks and
whites, anticolonialists and colonized. In an effort to unify this
broad constituency, the party simultaneously inaugurated a
campaign to promote what it had come to call "people's culture." On February 14, 1936, a coalition of black groups met in
Chicago at the National Negro Congress and vowed to support black artists who challenged stereotypical representations
of black people. This effort, called the Negro People's Front,
included a number of organizations, individuals, and institutions from diverse ideological beliefs: churches, civil rights organizations, black women's clubs, fraternal groups, politicians,
students, union members, and the black press. Although 1939
marked the official end of the party's Popular Front period, the
idea of a Popular Front would continue throughout the war
years. Without Popular Front venues like the Café Society, or
publications such as *PM*, a leftist newspaper, it is doubtful that
Petry, Primus, and Williams could have met with such success.
Popular Front initiatives focused on culture as an especially
important forum for educating and mobilizing audiences in
support of an antifascist agenda.[1]

Ann Petry and Mary Lou Williams were part of what one of
America's most important philosophers, Richard Rorty, identified as the Reformist Left, though he did not name either of
them as being members of that group. According to Rorty, the
Reformist Left included a diverse array of Americans who

fought within the framework of constitutional democracy to ensure the rights of the nation's weakest citizens. Such activists represented a broad range of progressive stances, from those calling themselves communists and socialists to those who eschewed political labels altogether.[2]

Borrowing a phrase from writer James Baldwin, Rorty used the term "achieving our country" to explain the work of the Reformist Left. This group of progressive intellectuals, artists, and activists sought to make the nation live up to its founding principles of liberty and equality for all. While they did not forget the brutality of our nation's past, they maintained that it was a continuous work in progress, one that had demonstrated and would continue to demonstrate its ability to become a better place.[3]

The three women of *Harlem Nocturne* sought to achieve America by directly confronting its legacy of white supremacy. Primus, Petry, and Williams consistently confronted the darkness of our nation's soul. They were critical of white supremacy and the excesses of American capitalism. Yet, their art and their activism also denoted a firm belief in the transformative nature of social change. They were agents, not spectators. They advocated for access to education, jobs, and adequate food and shelter. They were concerned with both racial and economic equality. They walked the streets of Harlem during the time that a young Baldwin walked those same streets. They saw what he saw, were angered and inspired by the people, forces, and sensibilities that would give rise to his own sense of rage, purpose, and justice. As with Baldwin, these women were not willing to forget or wholly forgive America's historical transgressions, but they were devoted to helping this nation "achieve" itself. They did so in a variety of ways and in a variety of contexts.[4]

The Communist Party was one venue through which some Americans tried to help their nation "achieve" itself. Pearl Primus was a member of the Communist Party. Of the three women, she was the most articulate about the struggle to make the United States a true democracy; for her the racial problem in America was a problem of democracy. All three women were politically engaged, though to differing degrees and along different points of the spectrum. Primus was the most politically radical of the three, sitting at the nexus of the Reformist Left and the Black Radical tradition. Although she worked for change within US borders, her concerns were always transnational, extending beyond the boundaries of the United States to include Africa and the Caribbean.[5]

Williams was rumored to have hosted Communist meetings in her apartment; she often offered her home up as a kind of intellectual and artistic salon to the people and causes she loved, admired, and supported. She was never a member of the party. Williams, long before her conversion to Catholicism, was instead largely driven by spiritual concerns that informed her strong sense of social justice. Petry was an editor of the *People's Voice*, and in that position she was surrounded by Communists. While she had respect and admiration for individual Communists, she protested any attempt to categorize her as such. She discounted the centrality of Marx to her own thinking, noting instead that biblical ethics informed her sensibilities. Whereas Williams sincerely sought meaning in her sense of spirituality, Petry may have been seeking to demonstrate the way her political views were steeped in values of the Judeo-Christian tradition that preceded Marxism, and would have distanced herself from the kind of radical politics that eventually fell out of favor.

Although each of these women lived in Harlem at some point during the period under consideration, their work took them throughout the entire city and ultimately throughout the nation and the world. By following them as they navigate Manhattan, we acquire a unique vision of the city during and immediately following World War II. New York sits at the center of this narrative. The city enabled and influenced their creativity. It facilitated their emergence as significant artists. It provided the social, cultural, and political context that laid the foundation for their careers.

In the 1940s, Harlem and New York were vibrant, glamorous, and exciting places, brimming with creativity. A new generation of artists ushered the transition from swing to bebop, tended the birth of rhythm and blues, questioned the continuing significance of social realism, experimented with abstraction, and sought a seat at the center of the national narrative. The forties differed from the better-known Harlem Renaissance and the Jazz Age in a number of important ways. Although the Harlem Renaissance produced Zora Neale Hurston, Nella Larsen, Jessie Fauset, Bessie Smith, and Josephine

Baker, among others, each of these women found her voice—
or her stride—in an earlier time, and black women never received as much attention and acclaim for their work as they
did during World War II. Furthermore, many of the women
who emerged during the forties more explicitly linked their
art and their public profile to a political movement.

Other women's voices contributed to this generational shift
as well: the poets Gwendolyn Brooks and Margaret Walker,
entertainers Hazel Scott and Lena Horne, and dancer Katherine Dunham, for instance. Lady Day was the Queen of 52nd
Street, and Ella Fitzgerald was "Flying Home." Sarah Vaughan,
first hired as a pianist for Earl "Fatha" Hines, soon left to join
Billy Eckstine's band with Miles Davis, Kenny Dorham, Art
Blakey, Lucky Thompson, Gene Ammons, and Dexter Gordon. And then there was the new queen of the blues, queen of
the black jukebox, Miss D herself—Dinah Washington, whose
Chicago-inflected, Harlem-based sound reflected the national
postwar optimism and a newfound African American confidence. Through their art, Ann Petry, Mary Lou Williams, and
Pearl Primus documented these times and in so doing helped
to shape the history of a city and its people by presenting per-
spectives that were absent from official records.

New York fed each woman's art, providing inspiration, material, and venues for performance and publication. However,
the city was no utopia; nor was it free of obstacles to black freedom. As late as 1940, 90 percent of New York State's defense
plants refused to hire black workers. The nearby Fox Hills
Army Camp in Staten Island was a segregated military base.

Furthermore, a number of restaurants and bars did not serve black patrons. Though subjected to these laws and customs, none of the women examined in this book lived racially segregated lives. Each claimed black and white friends, and Primus and Williams especially operated in racially integrated milieus. The tension between these restrictions and the sense of possibility with which they lived their own lives made them acutely aware of and committed to fighting against racial injustice.[6]

Despite the obstacles they endured in New York, these women were prominent artists. Through major works they also gave back to the city that enabled their art. Pearl Primus danced for soldiers and students. She became a favorite of *New York Times* dance critic John Martin, who covered all of her performances and, as a respected arbiter of taste, helped to cement her reputation. Among black dancers, only Katherine Dunham rivaled her. Ann Petry sits alongside Richard Wright and before Ralph Ellison and James Baldwin; through her work she presented complex, engaging, working-class black women in American fiction for the first time. She provided one of the first fully imagined portrayals of working-class Harlem in her 1946 novel *The Street*, which became the first book by a black woman to sell 1 million copies; it was widely reviewed in the black, left, and mainstream press. Mary Lou Williams became a major figure in the birth of bebop and challenged notions that women contributed to jazz only as vocalists. She was not simply the nurturing "godmother" of younger musicians such as Thelonious Monk and Bud Powell. In 1945, she had her own weekly radio broadcast, *Mary Lou Williams's Piano*

Workshop, and premiered her *Zodiac Suite* to diverse audiences at two of the city's most prestigious venues: Town Hall and Carnegie Hall.

All three women volunteered for causes they believed in, organized people and events, and taught younger artists. Their art was driven by a fierce passion for social justice and an insistent drive to create. Petry, Primus, and Williams were also included in anthologies and performances with some of the brightest talents of their generation. Their names frequently appeared in the press, and they were well known to culturally literate New York audiences.

Who were these women? Where did they acquire their confidence and their ambition? As was the case with many other American women, their youth, their marital statuses, and the absence of children gave them the freedom to focus on their careers. Petry and Williams were both in their early thirties during the war years, while Primus was in her early twenties. During this time none of them had children. Both Petry and Primus later became mothers, with one child each, but Williams remained childless throughout her life. Petry was married, but her husband was away at war for most of the time under consideration. Williams was separated from her second husband, the trumpeter Harold Baker, and Primus would not marry until the end of the decade.

Each of these women was highly intellectual and had prepared well for the path she pursued. Petry and Primus had gone to college. Williams, a child prodigy who began playing piano by ear at age two, went on the road before completing her formal education, but as the pianist, composer, and arranger for one of the most famous swing bands of the day (the Andy Kirk Orchestra), she was highly trained in her medium. All were avid readers and deep thinkers. In many ways each benefited from the struggles to open doors of opportunity for women and African Americans that had taken place during the earlier decades of the twentieth century. They all were cosmopolitan sophisticates, and before the end of their lives, they all had international reputations (Williams and Primus even lived outside of the United States for extended periods). They were recognized for their contributions to the arts. Unlike so many women artists, none of them died unappreciated and unknown. This is largely due to the efforts of members of younger generations, themselves inspired by the social movements of the sixties, especially the Black Power and Black Arts movements and the feminist movement, who, in their own search for foremothers, rediscovered these three pioneers.

By the early 1950s, the window of opportunity that had given these women the freedom to flourish had been shut, as Cold War politics and anti-Communist fervor took aim at the institutions that had supported them. Faced with these new limitations, each woman eventually left New York. Petry returned to Old Saybrook with her husband to raise her daughter. She would write two more novels, a number of short stories, and several books for children and young adults. Mary Lou Williams went to Paris, where, following a religious conversion, she gave up playing and composing music until she was encouraged to do these things again by her spiritual mentors. She returned to New York in the mid-1950s and eventually experienced a career resurgence in the 1970s. Williams continued to be involved with the most innovative forms of music until her death. With the rise of McCarthyism, Primus came under governmental surveillance. A grant from the Julius Rosenwald Foundation allowed her to travel to West Africa, and for the rest of her career she devoted her efforts to bringing West African dance to the world stage.

While the anti-Communist furor did not target Petry or Williams, by targeting the institutions, venues, and individuals supporting their art, it nevertheless helped to destroy the milieu that nurtured them. However, during the war years and the years immediately thereafter, each woman produced vibrant, creative, and important work that spoke to the centrality of humanity, documented its suffering and striving, and insisted upon a world where both justice and beauty could thrive.

Herein, these three women's stories are told in terms of "movement" in its multiple meanings. Literally, it means a change in position or place, as in the movement of those black and Latino people who were migrating to New York in record numbers. "Movement" is also an important concept in the arts, one that applies to diverse art forms. In dance it may simply mean a change of position or posture, a step or a figure. In music it signifies the transition from note to note or passage to passage, or it may refer to a division of a longer work. In literature, "movement" signals the progression or development of a plot or a storyline. Finally, there is the "political movement," defined as a series of actions on the part of a group of people working toward a common goal. Black people were on the move in the 1940s, migrating, marching, protesting, walking, dancing. These artists sought to imbue their work with this sense of mobility as well.

Harlem Nocturne moves through time by opening each chapter with an event from the year 1943 and following each woman through decade's end. The year 1943 was pivotal for many reasons in the lives of the women and in the life of the nation. Each woman experienced a major event that year: Primus appeared before thousands of spectators at the Negro Freedom Rally, Petry lived through the Harlem Riots, and Williams moved to New York. It was also the year that saw race riots in Los Angeles; Beaumont, Texas; and Detroit and coincided with the height of World War II. Each chapter focuses on one representative work of the period and closes with the artist's departure from New York, as late as 1952 when Williams set sail for Europe. Throughout, we walk, ride the subway, and dance with them.

And yet, oddly enough, as much as the times and the women themselves experienced multiple meanings of movement, there was also a sense of confinement that was evident in their lives and their work. Primus and Petry both confronted and challenged the debilitating limits of Jim Crow. The social movements of which they were a part faded away. In the case of Primus, she was constantly under surveillance, and her passport was revoked, thus severely limiting her own freedom of movement. This was a central paradox of the times: confinement within mobility—a frustrating tension that characterizes the narrative of black life in the United States.

Nonetheless, the benefit of hindsight shows us that though slow and incremental, the change for which Primus, Petry, and Williams fought and yearned continued to unfold. Hindsight also teaches us of the continued need for the kind of commitment, dedication, and discipline demonstrated by the women of *Harlem Nocturne*.

CHAPTER ONE

PEARL PRIMUS: DANCING FREEDOM

O n June 7, 1943, as World War II raged overseas, over 20,000 people gathered at Madison Square Garden for the second annual Negro Freedom Rally. Most of them came to be entertained, but they also had a sense of the event's importance: a communal call to fight Hitler abroad and Jim Crow at home. The rallies, the brainchild of A. Philip Randolph, embodied the Double V Campaign, which had mobilized urban communities nationwide. They celebrated black participation in the war effort and called for racial and economic equality in the United States. With the outbreak of World War II, black Americans saw a particular irony in the continued existence of racial discrimination and segregation within the nation's borders, even as black soldiers risked their lives in a war against fascism abroad.

During World War I, black leaders had called upon black Americans to support the war effort and had suspended vociferous protests against racial inequality. They hoped that by demonstrating their patriotism, they would convince whites to grant them full citizenship rights. Nowhere was this tactic more enthusiastically endorsed than in W. E. B. Du Bois's famous editorial in a 1918 issue of *The Crisis*, "Close Ranks," in which he encouraged black Americans to forget "their special grievances and close our ranks . . . with our fellow white citizens" in the fight for democracy. But the tactic failed. Upon their return, black soldiers met with racist violence, sometimes while still in their uniforms. Jim Crow continued to thrive, and racial injustice had not lessened.[1]

In light of the unsuccessful approach taken during World War I, a new militancy animated black American politics at the dawn of World War II. Led by the black press, especially the *Pittsburgh Courier*, black Americans embraced the call for Double V: victory against fascism abroad and racial inequality at home. But not all black Americans threw their support behind the campaign. Some black Communists, following the Communist Party's lead, rejected Double V as a distraction from the defeat of European fascism. At the other extreme, a small number of black Americans would reject any display of patriotism, believing the country to be incapable of fully accepting its black citizens. Nonetheless, the majority embraced the sentiments, if not the slogan, of Double V.

Double V would become a successful campaign both politically and economically, and its achievements, including those attained by the Fair Employment Practices Commission (FEPC), would translate into greater opportunities for black men and women. At each Freedom Rally, leaders showcased their successes. They crowned a "Miss Negro Victory Worker," awarding her with a war bond and large bouquet of flowers— with this one gesture highlighting black patriotism and celebrating their victories. The FEPC now required all businesses with government contracts to have a nondiscrimination clause, for example—and many black women took advantage of these new opportunities. Large numbers of them left domestic service and farm labor for factory work. The majority of them held only the most menial janitorial positions, but a few worked as riveters and welders, and a number of them worked as sewing-machine operators.[2]

At the 1943 rally, the audience heard Adam Clayton Powell Jr. deliver a rousing speech. Powell, a beloved son of Harlem, was a dynamic city councilman and a candidate for the US House of Representatives. He had announced his bid for Congress at the 1942 rally, telling his audience, "And it is because of the new Negro that I must, regardless of the time and energy or previous commitments, run for the Congress of the United States, so that we may have a national voice speaking from the national capital. . . . It doesn't matter what ticket or what party—my people demand a forthright, militant, anti–Uncle Tom congressman!"[3] "The New Negro" was a phrase used by each postslavery generation of black Americans to distinguish themselves from their forebears. The best-known use of the term emerged from the Harlem Renaissance. Powell's New Negroes were urban, politically empowered, and insistent upon their rights as citizens. They were no longer trying to prove their value or their worth to the white majority; instead, they were the avant-garde of American political culture, leading the way for their fellow citizens. Powell embodied the militancy and confidence that characterized a new generation of black Americans. He became the first black American to serve in Congress since the failure of Reconstruction. As pastor of the Abyssinian Baptist Church—one of black America's most highly regarded pulpits—Harlem community leader, and New York City councilman, he directly confronted racist hiring and housing policies. He had proven himself to be both fearless and ambitious.

The multitalented Paul Robeson was also on the bill. His dignified performance of "Water Boy," "Joe Hill," and "Ol' Man River" was a high point of the evening. Robeson had performed "Ol' Man River," by Jerome Kern and Oscar Hammerstein II, in various productions of the musical *Show Boat*. He recorded it in 1928 and sang it so often that it became one of his signature tunes. The song expresses the resilience of black people in the face of their ongoing struggles. "Joe Hill" is a tribute to the labor activist of the same name who was executed in 1915. "Water Boy," composed by Jacques Wolfe, is based on a traditional African-American prison work-song. All three songs were part of Robeson's repertoire.

By 1943 Robeson was internationally known as an artist and activist. An accomplished athlete, singer, and actor, the intellectually gifted Robeson was also a fiercely articulate leftist critic of racism and fascism. Throughout the war he lent his talents to the Allied forces. Less than a decade following his appearance at the Freedom Rally, the US government successfully targeted him as a Communist, dismantled his reputation, and purposefully contributed to his mental and physical demise. But in 1943, Robeson was still a hero to generations of young Americans. Following Robeson, a young woman, dark brown in color—small, but muscular—appeared onstage. Turning slowly, dramatically, she wrapped her arms around her body. Twisting left, then right, she lunged forward gracefully. But it was the leap, a jump of almost five feet that sent her soaring high above the rafters, which elicited gasps of astonishment from the audience. Treading air, the dancer seemed to linger there, in flight. It was this leap for which she would be remembered.

The audience would have been familiar with modern dancer Katherine Dunham or tap dancer Bill "Bojangles" Robinson, two of the most popular black dancers of the 1940s, but Pearl Primus, at twenty-four, was still relatively unknown. Readers of the *New York Times* or the *Amsterdam News* may have read about this young woman, this incredible emerging artist. By the time she performed at future Freedom Rallies in 1944 and 1945, she was a star. But on this afternoon in 1943, she sat at the precipice of an extraordinary career.

Primus danced to two recordings by Josh White, "Hard Time Blues" and "Jim Crow Train." "Hard Times Blues" is a song about black sharecroppers and their dispossession. In "Jim Crow Train," by Waring Cuney, White's guitar emulates the sound of a train in motion to lyrics expressing longing for the end of Jim Crow. Both were dances of social protest. With "Jim Crow Train," Primus carried her audience's frustrations

and aspirations within her body. She danced the confining, sti-
fling nature of segregation and then she leapt high above the
bleachers, right out of the imagined train. It was a leap of frustration, anger, and protest. When finally she flew, she took her
audience with her. Through physical movement, she sought to
inspire social and political movement. Years later, in 1978,
writing in her PhD dissertation about community responses
to great dancers in traditional West African societies, she may
well have been describing herself: "When these people truly
dance, there can be no observers. . . . [The observers] are
snatched, plucked up by an invisible force and hurled into the
ring of the dance, their own heartbeat matching the crescendo
of pulsing sound, their bodies becoming one with the sweat-
ing dancers."[4]

In his *Chicago Defender* column, the revered poet Langston
Hughes wrote: "Every time she leaped, folks felt like shouting.
Some did. Some hollered out loud."[5]

On this night Primus began to live out her calling: to use the
language of dance to represent the dignity and strength of black
people and to express their longing for freedom. Primus saw
dance as a means of contributing to the ongoing struggle for
social justice. The politically conscious young dancer had
learned that the dancer's movement has the power to transform
the observer's consciousness. This was a central component of
the aesthetic that informed her practice—a component she inherited from a tradition of vernacular dance born of Africa, and
one that was also central to modern dance itself. In fact, the
great modern dance critic and Primus champion John Martin
insisted that "movement . . . in and of itself is a medium for the

transference of an aesthetic and emotional concept from the consciousness of one individual to that of another."[6]

Modern dance had been ensconced in radical politics since its formation; traditional African dance sought to give expression to the community's history and aspirations. In creating a dialogue between these two forms, Primus helped to introduce a new context for the marriage of black aesthetics and politics. For Primus, traditional African dance and contemporary black vernacular dance were more than mere inspirations for modernist choreography; they were equal participants in helping to create a modern dance vocabulary.

Dance provided a new medium for the expression of protest against segregation, and it was a particularly effective challenge, in that dance is not bound by one or two dimensions. The dancer can move across planes of space; she can lie flat on the ground, writhing. She can stand flatfooted, twisting her body, arms wrapped around her torso and then flung outward toward her audience, before reaching up. And she can defy gravity, leave the ground, shoot into the air, into space. Primus's leaps were not those of a ballet dancer. Her body in the air looked like an abstract sculpture, exhibiting both strength and beauty. Her joints bent to create ninety-degree angles: the right knee might bend, the calf forming a line underneath her torso, while her left leg stretched out, ending in a pointed toe, arms parallel to her legs. Her leaps were not only meant to demonstrate grace but also to celebrate strength. However, they were not mere demonstrations of athleticism; they were fundamental to her choreography. They marked rhythm, moved her across the stage, and shot her up above it.

Pearl Primus in *Folk Dance* (1945). Photo by Gerda Peterich.

Through dance, Primus was able to portray the challenges and restrictions of segregation, and in her performance of "Jim Crow Train," she limned the walls of the Jim Crow car, made palpable its confining nature, and then resisted its constraints by leaping out of it, by flying rather than riding. In these choreographed gestures she embodied a particularly black paradox: forced confinement *and* forced mobility. While the major experience of black diasporic communities has been one of mobility, migration, and dislocation, these populations have also experienced forced confinement in various forms of segregation, imprisonment, and enslavement. Black activists and writers had been resisting segregated transportation since its institutionalization in 1893. In fact, for writers such as W. E. B. Du Bois and Charles Chesnutt, the Jim Crow car had become a major signifier of black people's second-class status. And both Ida B. Wells and Homer Plessy filed suits against segregated seating on public trolley cars to contest this second-class status. The blatant indignities of the Jim Crow car gave African Americans an opportunity to raise questions of class differences between black and white Americans, to challenge the social construction of race, and to question the ethics of white men who used the car to smoke, curse, and harass black women. For black women activists, the Jim Crow car was the impetus behind their challenge to race-based definitions of the term "lady." On some segregated cars, black women were forced from the "Ladies Car" to the "Smoker's Car" or the "Colored Car." Black women were excluded from the category "lady," and thus from the protections afforded by that term.[7]

At the time of her appearance at the Freedom Rally, Primus had never been on a Jim Crow car. She had been born in the Caribbean and had migrated to New York as a toddler, so she had missed the worst of southern racism. But much of her audience and many of her neighbors were migrants from the South and had experienced Jim Crow cars and other types of segregation firsthand. Between 1916 and 1930, approximately 1.5 million African Americans moved to northern cities in response to the call for wartime labor. This mass movement was known as the Great Migration. The Second Great Migration was longer and more sustained than the first. Between 1940 and 1970, over 5 million black southerners migrated north and west.

During this period, black Americans became an urban people. Large numbers of black migrants who now populated northern cities and lived in communities like Harlem and Bedford-Stuyvesant attended events such as the Freedom Rally. They brought with them firsthand knowledge of the indignities of racial segregation. Although black migrants had escaped the most persistent and virulent forms of racism, they carried their experiences with them when they left the South. Those experiences shaped their sense of history, culture, tradition, and family. For many, the South was *the* site of struggle, the primary but not the only battleground in the war against white supremacy. The North, they soon learned, was yet another battleground, and there they experienced a subtler and more insidious form of racism. There were no "Whites Only" signs in New York, but black migrants were racially segregated by neighborhood, and there were many establishments where they were not welcome. The existence of racial segregation struck many as a mockery of American ideals of democracy. They were joined by a growing number of white Americans who also believed the time had come to end Jim Crow. Many of them had also experienced segregated transportation: they rode in the "Whites Only" car.

As black and white Americans in cities like New York were confronted again and again with the failures of American democracy, they began to become more politically active. As a young dancer in New York, Primus tapped into that activism, creating pieces inspired by the black struggle in the United States. But she was also creating a repertoire based on African and Caribbean dance. As such, she constructed a vision of the African diaspora, one that was enabled not only by her own background but also by New York City. The city was an aspiring dancer's dream. There, Primus had access to folk and modern dance classes, to venues for social dance, such as Harlem's famous Savoy Ballroom, and to performances by dancers as diverse as Martha Graham and Asadata Dafora. In fact, she would dance with both of these pioneers. A native of Sierra Leone, Dafora—drummer, singer, and dancer—introduced African drumming and dance to the United States in the early 1930s. His 1934 performance of *Kykunkor* brought West African music and dance to the American concert stage. Martha Graham is one of the foremothers of modern dance in America, credited with having invented an entirely new movement vocabulary.

Primus was also exposed to a dance aesthetic that connected modern dance to social protest. Speaking about her preparation for the Negro Freedom Rally, she told the *Daily Worker:* "I know we must all do our part in this war to beat Fascism and I consider the battle against Jim Crow in America part of that fight, which is taking place on the battlefronts of the world." In this broad battle, Primus believed her dancing could serve as a tool to help dismantle these evils. She continued, "Each one of us can wield a weapon against Jim Crow and Fascism and my special one is dancing. I shall continue to protest Jim Crow through my dancing until Victory is won." Primus's statement demonstrates her grounding in Double V discourse linking fascism abroad with Jim Crow at home. According to Double V, both Nazism and Jim Crow were animated by white supremacist ideology and maintained by law and violence.[8]

The Popular Front aesthetic would also have a profound influence on the young dancer. The Popular Front, the coalition of liberals and leftists who opposed fascism, and the modern dance companies it inspired insisted that art, including dance, could be a weapon in the struggle for social justice. In the 1940s, Primus believed the arts were a tool in the struggle. Later, she recalled that "in the forties you could protest[;] in fact, I was most encouraged." She was not alone—Katherine Dunham and Talley Beatty also choreographed dances of social protest—but she was unique. Primus combined athleticism and grace, intellect and political passion, and had a devotion to the African past and present as well as a thorough engagement with the modernist aesthetic. She was less interested in commercial or popular success than Dunham and Beatty were; she was an intellectual first and foremost. For Primus, dance was as much a medium of teaching and consciousness raising as it was a form of entertainment—if not more so.[9]

Primus was not only engaged in a leftist political and artistic community, however; she was also part of a group of New York–based artists who wished to bring the culture of Africa and peoples of African descent to the attention of white audiences. Instead of evolving from a leftist to a black nationalist, instead of transitioning from an artist interested in social realism and modern dance to one interested in what would later be called "Afrocentricity," Primus always merged these political stances and aesthetic commitments. She did so by situating African dance alongside modern dance, and in so doing creating a dialogue between the two forms, showing them both to be representations of a longing for freedom and human dignity. In this way she was not different from a number of her politically engaged contemporaries. Long before her first trip to Africa in 1948, Primus was as interested in the history and culture of the continent as she was in the innovations of modern dance. In fact, her awareness of and interest in Africa preceded any formal dance training.[10]

When Primus told her own story, she almost always started with her Ashanti grandfather, who was a "voodoo" drummer in Trinidad, and with the masked, dancing figure of Carnival. She rooted her own artistry in her African and Caribbean roots. Her grandfather, "Lassido" Jackson, traced his lineage to an

Ashanti king. According to Primus, "he lived the life of a traditional person." She later said, "My home was an African
home."[11] Outside her childhood home, she recalled as an
adult, one could experience Harlem or Brooklyn, but inside,
it was always the Caribbean and Africa. As in the homes of
many black people, dance was not something to be performed
onstage, but something done in the home and in the ballroom. At times she claimed her mother excelled as a graceful
and gifted dancer. The dances at home or in the ballroom were
an amalgamation of Africa, the Caribbean, the American
South, and the black North. When Primus began her formal
training and then her professional career, she sought to dance
Africa, the Caribbean, and the American South as she imagined them and reconstructed them from her own research.
She danced this geography before she traveled it.

As a Caribbean immigrant to New York, Primus inherited a
legacy that combined political radicalism, pride in African an-
cestry, and a belief in the opportunities available to her in her
new home. She was one of the 40,000 Caribbean immigrants
who came to New York and Harlem between 1900 and 1930.
They were central to the development of Harlem's political and
artistic culture during this time. Primus inherited not only a
sense of culture from her Caribbean roots, but also a very
strong black nationalist worldview. Her father and uncle constantly talked of black nationalist leader Marcus Garvey and
his Back-to-Africa movement. She was aware of herself as an
African in the West, part of a people who had contributed
much to the development of the Americas, and part of a generation that would help to defeat fascism.[12]

Pearl Eileen Primus was born in Woodstock, Port of Spain, Trinidad, in 1919. In 1921 she and her mother joined her father in New York, part of a wave of Caribbean immigrants who settled in the city. Between 1913 and 1924, the peak years of Caribbean migration to the United States, large numbers of migrants settled in Manhattan and Brooklyn. By 1930, Caribbean immigrants made up a quarter of black Harlem's population. In New York, Primus, her parents, and her two brothers, Edward Jr. and Carl, first lived on 69th and Broadway, an area near what is now Lincoln Center. The neighborhood was home to a number of West Indian and African American families, including that of a budding young pianist named Thelonious Monk. Later, the Primuses moved to 110 East 97th Street, between Park and Lexington Avenues in East Harlem. Although the area housed a number of black families, it would soon be best known for its Puerto Rican inhabitants. Even in the thirties, this part of Harlem was more ethnically and racially diverse than its better-known western side. Eventually, the Primus family would move to another Caribbean stronghold in Brooklyn, Bedford-Stuyvesant.[13]

Like many other Caribbean immigrants of this first major wave, the Primus family put a high premium on education and professional achievement. Therefore it is not surprising that Pearl attended one of the city's most competitive high schools, Hunter College High School. Founded to teach intellectually gifted girls, Hunter College High School was established as a private girls' school in 1896. It eventually became a selective magnet public school, but it was not operated by the New York City Department of Education; instead, it was administered by

Hunter College. Primus was one of the few black students to attend. After graduating from Hunter College High School, Primus enrolled at Hunter College, where she was a pre-med and biology major. The college was open to all qualified young women regardless of religion or ethnicity, and it maintained a reputation for a rigorous program of academic study.

Although she aspired to be a doctor, Primus had a broad range of interests as a student. She was an Olympic-caliber track-and-field star who excelled at the broad jump; she minored in physical education and took classes in dancing, apparatus, fencing, basketball, tennis, and possibly swimming ("if I can get it," she wrote in her journal before registration). Even as early as 1937, she wrote, "I'd love to specialize in the dancing but it is not stressed more than the others."[14] That she majored in biology and excelled at sports would not be insignificant. She understood, both intellectually and experientially, the mechanics of the body. But although she was an avid athlete and dancer, at this time in her life Primus seemed destined to be a scientist.

Still, her letters and journal entries from this period reveal a sensitive, thoughtful, intellectually curious young woman devoted to her family, her studies, and her friends. She possessed a poetic nature and a love of the natural world and the changing seasons. A well-rounded reader, she was also ambitious, hoping to earn a PhD in biology and eventually to become a surgeon. As Hunter was a commuter school, Primus lived at home with her close-knit family. In one journal entry from that time, she described her chaotic room as she studied for finals:

"All my biological instruments, frogs, skeletons, butterflies, glass jars, stirring rod, mixing bowls, hard lens, all my drawing apparatus, chalks and rags; all my school notes . . . my books are now arranged under the bed."[15]

The young Primus also took full advantage of New York, catching shows and visiting museums. In another journal entry she noted her excitement that *Richard II* was scheduled to re-open soon and said that she "would also like to hike thru Tibbetts Brook Park. I want to see the Frick Collection too."[16] Tibbetts Brook Park, which opened in 1927, is a large park located in Yonkers, only a few miles north of Manhattan, and it provided nature-loving New Yorkers like Primus with the opportunity to hike and fish. On the opposite end of this bucolic setting, the Frick Collection, located on 70th Street between Madison and Fifth, housed major works of art by European artists. So the young woman who had been born in Trinidad became a true New Yorker as she explored the full range of what her city had to offer. She also went to the Savoy in Harlem, where she danced all the popular social dances and especially enjoyed the Lindy Hop. Perhaps she used her athletic skills as she leapt, keeping time with the music, soaring with, if not above, the other dancers. She even may have danced in a crowd that included Malcolm Little, later to become Malcolm X.

After graduating from Hunter College in 1940, Primus sought out work as a lab technician in order to earn money to attend Howard Medical School. However, because of racism, none of the labs to which she applied would hire her, despite her qualifications, and she was forced to take various clerical and menial jobs. She worked as a cherry picker, a riveter, a switchboard operator, a welder for Todd Shipyards in Hoboken, and a clerical worker at the National Maritime Workers Union.[17] Primus was one of a growing number of women who found work in the war industry, which was up and running as the famed "arsenal of democracy" as early as 1940. Women in New York could be found operating elevators, driving trucks and taxis, and "riveting, welding, and working the assembly line in war plants and in the Brooklyn Navy Yard." For the most part, black women still met with difficulty when they sought skilled labor or clerical work, which is why Primus could rarely find anything but unskilled jobs. Although Executive Order 8802, signed by President Roosevelt in June 1941, banned race discrimination in the defense industry, it was rarely enforced. Very few black women were as successful as Primus was in acquiring employment as welders or riveters.[18]

In 1941, Primus refocused her attention on her education and finally began to find work more suited to her interests. She began to pursue graduate classes in health education at New York University before transferring to a master's program in psychology at Hunter. That same year she found employment with the wardrobe department of the Depression-era National Youth Administration (NYA). Created in 1935, the NYA was a New Deal program designed to address the problem of unemployment among young Americans by offering grants to high-school and college students in exchange for work. For young people who were not enrolled in school and who were unemployed, the NYA offered on-the-job training on federally funded work projects. By 1937 there was also a special program for African Americans directed by Mary McLeod Bethune. Primus had taken dance classes throughout her time at Hunter, but the NYA provided her with her first opportunity to perform. She danced in a program entitled *America Dances*. With this performance she gained a number of admirers and supporters who encouraged her to continue with dance.

During this period, Primus also became involved with two institutions that would help to nurture her artistic and political visions. She worked as a counselor at Camp Wo-Chi-Ca (short for Workers Children's Camp), a leftist children's camp in rural New Jersey, and she auditioned for and was granted a scholarship to the New Dance Group's school. Founded in 1934, Camp Wo-Chi-Ca was fully integrated and offered scholarships to students who couldn't otherwise afford to attend. The young Primus was in fine company when she joined the staff of Camp Wo-Chi-Ca as a dance counselor. Visitors to the camp included the painter Charles White, the author Howard Fast, painter Jacob Lawrence, sculptor Augusta Savage, and poet Langston Hughes, and many of these artists would become Primus's friends and collaborators in later years. In fact, one of her charges was Paul Robeson Jr., son of the famed activist and performer. Primus taught the younger Robeson how to Lindy, and Robeson Sr. told her she was responsible for the holes in his rug, a result of countless hours of his son's practicing. The camp would gain attention in later years for its continued support of Paul Robeson when he was targeted as a Communist during the height of the McCarthy era.

The New Dance Group had been established in 1932 by artists dedicated to social change through dance, and its studio was the only place in New York where one could take racially integrated dance classes. However, the atmosphere among the students was not always welcoming. Primus was one of four selected to receive scholarships out of a total of twenty-seven dancers who auditioned for spaces; the "award" required her to do menial labor—washing floors and cleaning toilets—in exchange for two hours of instruction per week. At times white students would purposely bump into Primus on the studio dance floor. These small gestures of hostility were evidence of the racist indignities quietly suffered by black people in even the most liberal of settings. Still, Primus persevered, and her experiences as a student, a dancer, and a worker all helped to shape her art, her politics, and her philosophical outlook.

Young dancers at the New Dance Group were exposed to leftist and progressive political thought and activism, but Primus came to the school with her own progressive political principles. There she found an affirmation of her commitment to linking social change with modern dance. In addition to encouraging students to be cognizant of the relationship between politics and dance, the New Dance Group provided exquisite technical training. At their studios, Primus studied ballet, modern dance, tap dance, and cultural dances from other countries as well as dance history, philosophy, and choreography. She was taught by the leading luminaries of modern dance, including Martha Graham, Doris Humphrey, Charles Weidman, and Beryl McBurnie. Primus credited Weidman's work with "aiding me in the use of speed and distance on the stage."[19] McBurnie, also known as "La Belle Rosette," was a Trinidadian dancer and choreographer who also taught Katherine Dunham, Geoffrey Holder, and Primus's future husband, Percival Borde. Judith Delmer, the secretary of the New Dance Group, introduced Primus to African sculpture, from which the young dancer learned postures and angles. From photographs and collections of African art housed throughout the city, she made note of bodies leaning forward in relaxed stances, the connection of the feet to the earth, and the use of the free and relaxed hand.[20]

Primus soon became entrenched in the world of modern dance. She also quickly emerged as one of the city's most promising young dancers. On Valentine's Day 1943, she made her professional debut as part of a program at the 92nd Street Y entitled *Five Dancers*, featuring Nona Schurman, Gertrude Prokosch Kurath, Julia Levien, and Iris Mabry, all of whom would, like Primus, become major figures in modern dance performance and scholarship. There Primus premiered two solos, "African Ceremonial" and "Hear-de-Lans-a-Crying." It had taken her six months to research and create "African Ceremonial." In preparation, she read books, journals, and travel diaries. She looked at photos, paintings, and drawings in museums. She spoke with African graduate students and worked with Norman Coker, a dancer from West Africa who had worked with Asadata Dafora.[21]

Of *Five Dancers*, John Martin, dance critic at the *New York Times*, wrote: "If Miss Primus walked away with the lion's share of the honors, it was partly because her material was more theatrically effective, but also partly because she is a remarkably gifted artist." Martin went on to write that while Primus had been seen in New Dance Group productions and with Belle Rosette, she deserved a company of her own. Following her appearance at *Five Dancers*, the "audience literally yelled for more of her."[22]

What a debut! Martin, the most influential critic of modern dance, would become Primus's champion and adviser. In person, Martin encouraged her to pursue dance full-time, noting that through the dance she could also heal people. While he saw her as "the most gifted artist-dancer of her race," he also noted that "it would be manifestly unfair to classify her merely as an outstanding Negro dancer, for by any standard of comparison she is an outstanding dancer without regard for race."[23] Martin further raved, "She has tremendous inward power, a fine dramatic sense, a talent for comedy and, marvelous to relate, a really superb technique with which to eternalize them." When a critic of Martin's stature singles out a young dancer, others of power and influence take notice. Martin's personal encouragement and his published reviews nurtured the young dancer and helped to create audience curiosity and enthusiasm for her performances.

Martin, along with a number of other white critics, seemed to prefer Primus to Katherine Dunham. Dunham was the best-known black modern dancer for many years. Her shadow looms large. She is the point of comparison for all black dancers and choreographers who seek to make a name for themselves in the field of modern dance. Ten years Primus's senior, Dunham had founded her first company in 1937 and had begun researching dance in Haiti, Jamaica, Trinidad, Cuba, and Martinique in 1936. This research would ultimately culminate in

Pearl Primus, October 11, 1943. Photo by Carl Van Vechten.

the publication of numerous writings as well as the development of a movement vocabulary—the Dunham technique. The company gained a great deal of attention when it premiered at New York's Windsor Theater. By the year of Primus's debut, Dunham and her company had appeared in the films *Cabin in the Sky* and *Stormy Weather;* two years later, in 1945, she opened the Dunham School of Dance and Theater in New York. In order to fully appreciate Primus, it is important to understand what she shared with, and how she departed from, Dunham, who certainly blazed a path for her.[24]

Dunham and Primus were early recognized as important figures in dance. When Margaret Lloyd published *The Borzoi Book of Modern Dance* in 1949, the first major history of the form, she included sections on both dancers. In doing so, Lloyd acknowledged the significant contributions made by both dancers. She made note of their differences as well. Dunham brought a sense of showmanship, drama, and glamour to her performances of Caribbean-inspired dances. Critics found Dunham's choreography more sexual than Primus's, but Primus brought greater physical power to her movements. Primus presented African, Caribbean, and black American dances on the stage without glamorizing them and sought to use the stage to educate viewers about lesser-known histories and cultures. Many white critics, including Lloyd, seemed more comfortable with Primus; for them, she represented dance in its "authentic" form. It is unclear whether this was an estimation reserved for black dancers. Finally, unlike Dunham, Primus avoided personal contact with her audience. In this way, she was like her friend, pianist, composer, and arranger

Mary Lou Williams and other members of the young generation of emerging bebop musicians, all of whom sought to em-
phasize their identity as serious artists as much, if not more
so, than the role of entertainer. For some black women, in
particular, it was sometimes necessary to create a kind of self-
protective distance from an audience that might project fan-
tasies of sexual availability onto their performance.

While the black press appreciated what both Dunham and
Primus had to offer, Dunham received the lion's share of attention; she was the bigger and more accomplished star and an
outspoken critic of racial segregation. She also fit the standard
of beauty that dominated the black press. Dunham had her
own company, and her productions were more theatrical.
However, at least one article in the *Amsterdam News* applauded
Primus's seriousness over Dunham's turn to skimpy costumes
and Hollywood.[25]

Speaking of the difference between herself and Primus,
Dunham told an interviewer, "As far as some relationships
between our choreography, our work, our plans, or inten-
tions I don't think that exists. I think that Pearl Primus is
chiefly African oriented. I think she has done a great job in
bringing this to the American public. Whereas my work has
been much more Caribbean and eclectic." She went on to ob-
serve, "I would say my interest is not to reconstruct or present from an anthropologist point of view African material
and I admire Pearl Primus for this because that seems to be
her intention. I am more interested in what can I do cre-
atively with the material that comes from these backgrounds
that I am interested in."[26]

While there is an expression of mutual respect, there is no discussion of friendship or collaboration. Dunham seems to suggest that Primus is primarily interested in reproducing authentic African dance for American audiences, while she is inspired by dances of the diaspora to create something new. Ultimately, she is making a distinction between the academic and the artist, identifying herself as the latter. It is not a distinction Primus would likely have made. She saw herself as both scholar and artist. Her understanding of "artist" was not as the individual who stands apart from the community; instead, it was a role chosen by the ancestors and created for the community to embody its history, bear its culture, and provide it with a vision, a path, and capacity for the future.

Modern dance had emerged in the early twentieth century, and by the forties it still did not have the status of classical ballet. Modern dancers might appear on a concert stage on Tuesday and perform as part of a vaudeville review on Wednesday. Despite the fame her performance in *Five Dancers* brought her, Primus could not expect to make a living through modern dance alone. Unlike Dunham's own dance company, few modern dance companies were racially integrated. So, like many famed dancers, singers, and musicians of her generation, especially black artists, Primus entered the nightclub scene and began performing at the legendary Café Society.

Much has been written about Café Society. Founded by Barney Josephson, it opened in 1938 in Greenwich Village. The first racially integrated club in New York, Café Society quickly became a gathering place for liberal and leftist socialites, intellectuals, artists, and political activists. The club's reputation is well deserved when we consider the patrons and the artists who found their way there. The club was the site of political education for a number of artists as well as the venue where they found their individual creative voices. It is perhaps best known as the place where Billie Holiday introduced "Strange Fruit," but the club also helped to launch the careers of Lena Horne and Hazel Scott. Café Society lacked a chorus line and hatcheck girls; instead, it showcased comedians and vocalists, self-accompanying solo artists, an ensemble, a boogie-woogie pianist, a solo pianist, a dance orchestra, and sometimes, a dancer. Zero Mostel, Imogene Coca, Josh White, Teddy Wilson, Albert Ammons, and, after the summer of '43, Mary Lou Williams were but some of the artists who appeared there. John Hammond was the club's musical director. Its employees—cooks, waiters, musicians, and comedians—were all unionized.

The nightclub and its owner are just as well known for their leftist Popular Front politics as for the talent that appeared there. Indeed, the club was rumored to have started as a fund-raising vehicle for the Communist Party. Barney Josephson's brother was a noted member of the Communist Party, and Josephson himself remained under FBI surveillance for almost twenty years. Eventually, J. Edgar Hoover's obsession with routing out Communists would lead to the club's demise, but in the early 1940s it was still a breeding ground for politically minded artists and activists. On any given night, one might find Walter White, Ralph Bunche, Richard Wright, E. Franklin Frazier, Paul Robeson, Langston Hughes, or Sterling Brown in the audience. Adam Clayton Powell Jr. might drop in, especially when he began courting Hazel Scott, though he was married. One night Eleanor Roosevelt paid a visit. The Café Society audience was made up of intellectuals, writers, labor activists, jazz fans, students, and celebrities. One might find Nelson Rockefeller seated next to Charlie Chaplin, Errol Flynn, or Gene Kelley, or meet a young Betty Perske, on her way to becoming as famous as Lauren Bacall. Here was a gathering of Rorty's Reformist Left.[27]

In the spring of 1943, Primus successfully auditioned for Barney Josephson at Café Society Downtown. She had been working as a switchboard operator and going to school at the time, when a man on the street recognized her and said, "Hey, aren't you dat kid John Martin wrote about? What the hell are you doing here? Why don't you go down to Café Society?" She had never been to a nightclub before, though she had frequented the Savoy, where she danced the Lindy Hop. In an unpublished interview with Elsa Wren, Primus later recalled, "I had on a pale blue scarf, a pleated skirt, an organdy blouse and red shoes and socks." Josephson was not impressed. He had presented Billie Holiday, Lena Horne, and Hazel Scott, all of whom were known for their glamorous sophistication. Primus showed him her clippings and told him, "The person you see sitting here is not the person you'd see on stage, they are two completely different things." Josephson remembered, "You form an opinion when someone comes looking for a job, how they come dressed, how their hair is combed, wanting to make a good impression. This woman came in not really well-groomed, as if she just had not bothered getting herself ready for an audition. I was very unimpressed. I didn't know then that she was a graduate of Hunter College in biology and even then she was studying for her master's degree in psychology." He thought, "Oh god, I can't present anyone who looks like this."[28]

Josephson told her his record player wasn't working. "I just wanted to put her off. I didn't want to audition her. Well, she was tearful." After she told him she was working for the National Maritime Workers Union as a clerk and that she couldn't afford to take another day off from work, he agreed to see her dance. "She took one leap, one leg behind, both arms outstretched, I thought she'd go through the wall. Her legs were very muscular, like a man's legs, power like iron, and bronze, her color." Josephson preferred jazz tap dancing and cared little for ballet and modern dance, but admitted, "As little as I know about dance, and that was little enough, when I saw that leap I knew it was something. This woman, whom I had been trying to get rid of, knocked me off my ass."[29] He hired her on the spot to work at Café Society Downtown, and she opened in April for a ten-month engagement.

The reason Josephson did not find Primus physically attractive may have been that his notions of beauty were more along the lines of Lena Horne and Billie Holiday. Holiday noted that Josephson thought Hazel Scott was "too dark" until he heard her play. Eventually, Scott's talent won him over, and he would become physically attracted to her as well. She became his most successful star and the darling of Café Society Uptown. But soon Primus would herald a new kind of beauty for black women, one that would become common among modern

dancers and other bohemian artists, in particular. Primus recalled, "I had not, except in instances like Paul Robeson or
Marian Anderson or Billie Holiday, come across as a beautiful
woman because I was dark. . . . There were times, and I wore
my hair quite natural, when I was accosted on the streets and
those were the days when if you were fair you were bea-u-ti-ful
if your nose was a certain way, you were bea-u-ti-ful and that
was that."[30]

Dancers live in and are defined by their bodies, and Primus's
was the perfect body for the kind of dance that would ultimately call her. Beautiful and sculpted, with muscular quadri-
ceps that propelled her into the air when necessary, it was not
a body familiar to the Western concert stage. Katherine Dunham was considered the sultry beauty, but the press never
spoke of Primus in those terms. Instead, she was "strong,"
"powerful," "earthy," "stocky," "pure." In 1947, *Time* magazine
identified her as "a squat, powerful Negro girl." Four years later,
the same magazine called her "a stocky, powerhouse dancer."[31]
In the earlier article, Primus described herself: "My body is
built for heavy stomping, powerful dignity." On the pages of
grant-making reports or even mainstream publications, her
body was often described as "heavy," even "overweight," although she weighed only 115 pounds in her twenties. Even her
contemporaries made note of her body. Dancer and dance his-
torian Joe Nash recalled, of his first meeting with her, "This
short, dark skinned girl . . . she didn't have the body of a
dancer." Another dancer, Muriel Mannings, noted, "Her body
was different than most dancers' bodies. She was chunky."[32]
A contemporary reader might be struck by the similarity of

adjectives used to describe Primus and tennis star Serena Williams, or former Olympic ice skater Surya Bonaly, both of whom are admired for their athleticism and power, but whose grace, femininity, and beauty have been questioned.

But Primus would pave the way for a different kind of physical type. If people like Josephson did not find her beautiful, some young women were inspired by her personal aesthetic. While a student at Primus's alma mater, Hunter College High School, where Primus came to speak, the young poet Audre Lorde sat mesmerized by Primus's tales of Africa—and her natural hair. Lorde left the auditorium and, on her way to her Harlem home, stopped in a barbershop and had her hair cut into a short natural style.

Black modern dancers would be among the first notable black women to wear their hair natural. The rigorous movement required of modern dancers made it difficult for them to maintain processed or straightened hair. For figures such as Primus, and later her student, a young Maya Angelou, unprocessed hair styles were born of necessity. Because these women carried themselves with an air of pride and confidence, their hair came to connote similar sentiments. They were among a rare group of black women who were able to defy convention and forgo straightening their hair. This would not be the case for the majority of black American women until the sixties. As late as 1966, Phyl Garland wrote an article in *Ebony* magazine about the new affinity for natural hair, citing Primus as an early champion: "This key element in the black female's mystique was, until recently, challenged only by a few bold bohemians, a handful of entertainers and dancing ethnologists like Pearl Primus, whose identification with the exotic placed them beyond the pale of convention." In this way Primus was a pioneer for women like Cicely Tyson, Abbey Lincoln, Miriam Makeba, and Nina Simone who would be purveyors of the new sensibility during the "Black is Beautiful" sixties.[33]

Nightly at Café Society Primus worked on her choreography. She found inspiration from other artists and made contacts for future performances and other venues. There she honed her craft and became a part of the community of artists who performed there. As Primus would later explain, "Cafe Society is the place where my discovery became more than a one night thing."[34] At Café Society, Primus met and befriended Josh White and Mary Lou Williams, and she would dance to songs created and performed by both of them. Josephson teamed her up with White for "Hard Time Blues," which Primus would perform at the 1943 Negro Freedom Rally. Williams, meanwhile, dedicated one part of her famed *Zodiac Suite*, "Capricorn," to Primus, and Primus danced to that piece as well.

The most important collaboration between Primus and Williams was a piece called "The Study in Nothing," which they performed on June 1, 1944, at Hunter College. They were both very serious artists, devoted to the development of their craft and the artistic expression of their ideas. Neither interacted playfully with her audiences, and for this, each would be criticized. Although both had experienced the sting of colorism in their own communities, Williams was the more glamorous of the two, with her thick, straightened hair and her beautiful gowns, minks, and extensive collection of shoes. But here, they came together as artists, and their relationship provided them the space to take risks, to be inventive, to explore, and even to be playful. The piece was a humorous duet with piano and offered the women an opportunity to produce something experimental, abstract, nonrepresentational, and nonracial. Significantly, they did not create a work about being black women. Their shared race and gender seem to have freed them to transcend both of those identities, if only momentarily, to explore a more abstract, aesthetic collaboration. Unfortunately, the performance was not recorded, but those who saw it described it as one individual responding to the sound of a singular musical note. Dancer and audience chased the sound.[35]

Collaborations like this one made Café Society the most important performance venue for Primus during this time in her career. Primus's seriousness, along with her ambition, may have made her a difficult person to work with, but numerous artists, including John Cage, Langston Hughes, Owen Dodson, Mary Lou Williams, and Josh White, nevertheless did collaborate with her. Cage composed "Our Spring Will Come" for his work with Primus. It was to have been accompanied by the recitation of a Langston Hughes poem. The John Cage Trust describes the piece as "a lively and rhythmically intense work, set in a kind of rondo form."[36] Josh White was a frequent collaborator with Primus. In addition to performing at Café Society together, White and Primus toured throughout the

Pearl Primus performs to "Honeysuckle Rose" as played by Teddy Wilson
(piano), Lou McGarity (trombone), Sidney Catlett (drums), Bobby Hackett
(trumpet), and John Simons (bass). For more information, see "Giants at Play: Life
with Jazz Legends," *Life*, Time Life Historic Moments (photo gallery), especially http://life
.time.com/culture/photos-of-jazz-legends-duke-ellington-billie-holiday-dizzy-and-more/#2.
Photo by Gjon Mili.

United States in the 1940s, and Primus would continue to include works set to his music in her repertoire for years to come.

At Café Society, Primus was ensconced in a community of innovative and politically minded artists, activists, and intellectuals who were open to new aesthetic expressions. She had found
encouraging supporters in Josephson and Martin. The club was
central to her ascendancy in 1943. In June, she made her show-
stopping leaps at the Negro Freedom Rally. In August, John

Martin named Primus "the most distinguished newcomer of the season," even though "there were more newcomers than usual in this wartime season." By the end of that year, Primus had choreographed and premiered a number of dances inspired by the works of other Café Society habitués. She choreographed "Strange Fruit" to Lewis Allan's poem, made famous in the 1939 song of the same title recorded by Billie Holiday.[37] She also choreographed "The Negro Speaks of Rivers," inspired by Langston Hughes's poem. Her photograph appeared in *Life* magazine, and she closed the year with a performance at the African Dance Festival at Carnegie Hall, where she appeared with Asadata Dafora. Eleanor Roosevelt was in attendance.

Like other artists committed to Double V during the height of the war, Primus used her art both to protest against racism and to demonstrate her support for the war effort. For instance, in addition to her concert performances, Primus often entertained the troops at USO events, later recalling that they loved her jazz dances the best. In fact, in 1944 she received a USO Certificate of Merit for entertaining servicemen in camps, hospitals, and ports of embarkation.[38]

Sometime during this period, Primus met a young Jewish man named Yael Woll. Though she seems to have left little time for a personal life, she would eventually marry him. Himself a leftist, Woll later recalled having met her in the early 1940s, most likely at an event or benefit where she performed. Few details about their relationship exist. When they married in 1950, few people in Primus's life seem to have known about it.

However, *Jet* magazine, in 1952, listed Primus, along with Lena Horne, Katherine Dunham, Hilda Simms, and Josephine Baker, as prominent black women who were married to white men. Woll, who later became a film and television director, worked closely with Primus, serving as a kind of stage manager during her tours. He seems to have been a very supportive husband. The two traveled together to Israel in 1952, where she performed and where the press referred to her as "Mrs. Yael Woll." Woll was apparently disappointed by her extended travel to Africa, which kept her away from home for months at a time. During one trip to Trinidad, while still married to Woll, Primus fell in love with the Trinidadian dancer Percival Borde. Primus often noted that she and Borde married in 1954, but she did not officially marry him until 1961. After that time, she rarely mentioned Woll. She basically erased him from her history, referring to Borde as her first and only husband.[39]

Prior to her first marriage, in the summer of 1944, Pearl Primus left New York to travel extensively throughout the Deep South in search of material for her dance. However, the trip yielded much more: it also strengthened her political resolve. This change would influence the way she portrayed these struggles. Of her travels in the South during this period, Primus later told the *Daily Worker:* "I am not trying to create something new in the dance. . . . I am only attempting to present the Negro in his own true light as he was in Africa and as he is now, a member of a fighting democracy."[40] Again, though dance is her medium, here she represents herself as a scholar or a journalist seeking to reveal the truth, rather than as a creative artist who is inspired by her findings. Primus highlights the dignity of the African past while calling attention to the black contribution to the most important struggle of modern times. She sought to present "Negroes" as people with a history as well as modern subjects, cocreators in contemporary civilization.

Primus did not romanticize southern life. Of the South, she wrote, "The Spanish moss hangs like a crepe over everything, is a fungus that creeps through everybody."[41] She wasn't nostalgic for a past that never was; nor did she look longingly to the South as a home, like many black migrants. Instead, she wanted to experience firsthand the land that informed the sensibilities of many of her contemporaries and audiences. A large number of African Americans living in northern cities were recent migrants who had come north during the Great Migrations, and she wanted to understand the world they had left behind.

Primus's trip to the South was an eye-opener for her. She didn't see a world of victims and villains: "I could not hate anyone," she later said. "It was a pathetic scene, both sides swallowed by fear of one another. Everything looked ugly to me there—the Negroes because of their hunger and feeling of inferiority, the whites because of their fear and hunger." Her experience was not one that made her fall in love with black southerners. Nor did it cause her to hate whites. In fact, a few encounters with whites made her question her own assumptions. When she started to faint in a Jim Crow bus, a white man got up and offered her his seat.[42]

Primus sought to know intimately the landscape and the people, so she disguised herself as a field worker, worked alongside sharecroppers, and visited their churches in the evenings and on the weekends. It was in church that she made note of the core rhythms of black music, oratory, and movement: the preacher's intonations were as rhythmic as the drum, his movements as dramatic and graceful as a dance. The congregation responded to him with tears, ecstatic movement—shouting and leaping from their seats. Primus observed leaps and crawling bodies, "snake-like undulations" not unlike the dances to the god Damballa in the Caribbean. She began to see connections between the Caribbean dances with which she was familiar and the movement she observed among former slaves in the South. She visited little churches and open-air prayer meetings in Georgia, Alabama, and South Carolina, and everywhere she observed similar kinds of movement.[43]

Primus had danced the part of a sharecropper in "Hard Time Blues" at the Negro Freedom Rally, but now she bore witness to their bodies and movements. During this trip, Primus joined a historic trail of black intellectuals whose first encounters with the American South would inform their artistic, intellectual, and political sensibilities forever. W. E. B. Du Bois, Jean Toomer, and the painter Eldzier Cortor, among others, undertook this "Journey of Immersion" before emerging as people who could articulate the concerns of American blacks and build upon both the pain and the beauty of life under Jim Crow. Langston Hughes and Zora Neale Hurston, who was born in Alabama and raised in Florida, left New York for extended forays into the South, a place believed to be the fount of African American culture. Primus would later say:

> If I were dancing about how sharecropping or how our spiritu-
> als came into being and what they mean in the lives of people
> or if I wanted to know the truth about the commissary stores
> that refused food to the people, then I wanted to know what
> they were like. . . . That's why I went south. I went south to live
> among the people and to be part of the cultures of the South-
> lands to know what cotton was. Except for the museum up
> here in New York . . . I didn't know what it was. . . . I did get
> into the fields and along the dockside and into the revival
> churches of the South. I walked those long dusty roads be-
> tween towns. So when I began to create about these experi-
> ences the remembered feelings were part of what I was
> speaking about. It wasn't that I'd read about it but that I had ex-
> perienced it.[44]

This would be the same reason she ultimately went to Africa: to move beyond reading in order to experience what her migrant audience had experienced; to witness and bear witness to what Du Bois had called, in the title of his 1903 book, the "Souls of Black Folk." She saw and placed movement in context. The trip to the American South was the first time she brought this kind of methodology to dance.

It was also during this period that Primus tied her political activism to the causes of the Southern Negro Youth Congress (SNYC). Founded in 1937, SNYC was an organization of young black activists who were devoted to guaranteeing and protecting the rights of southern blacks. They worked closely with a number of leftist and political organizations, black and white. According to her FBI file, Primus attended the organization's Leadership School in Atlanta from August 7 through August 18, 1944, right in the middle of her research trip. SNYC's Leadership Academies were held throughout the South. Prominent activists and educators attended the one in Atlanta, including Horace Mann Bond, an educator and leader who was also the father of civil rights activist Julian Bond. Primus would have joined students, people from the community, teachers, sharecroppers, and faculty members of neighboring black colleges for these classes.[45]

Given the nature of her research among southern sharecroppers, it is not surprising that Primus would have been moved by their condition and want to help alleviate their economic, social, and political sufferings. As an activist-minded artist, she would have been drawn to other courageous young people working to empower southern blacks. The young people of the Southern Negro Youth Conference represented a cross-section of the black community. Many, such as Esther Cooper Jackson, her husband James Jackson, and Louis and Dorothy Burnham, were college-educated young people from the North who came to Alabama to organize rural blacks. Esther Cooper Jackson received her bachelor's degree from Oberlin College and her master's in sociology from Fisk, where she wrote a thesis on organizing black domestic workers in New York. She was on her way to the University of Chicago for a PhD when she went to

Alabama to work on a SNYC voter registration drive. Other members of SNYC were young sharecroppers or factory workers. Still others were young southern students, such as Sallye Bell Davis, a Birmingham native and student at Miles College. Davis would give birth to radical activist Angela Davis.

Many of the members of SNYC were also members of the Communist Party. But, like those black Americans who were committed to Double V, who were more focused on waging national battles for equality and civil rights than on pursuing the goals of international communism, SNYC didn't have explicit ties to the Soviet Union. As Esther Cooper Jackson later asserted: "There wasn't anybody from Moscow telling us what to do." One of the organization's pamphlets said, "We Negro Youth act to win the full blessing of true democracy for ourselves, for our people, for our nation."[46] They were committed to the vision of an interracial society free of poverty and racism where all people would exercise their right to vote and have the opportunity to reach their full potential.

Because SNYC activists understood the centrality of the expressive arts to black Americans, they also placed a premium on the "unique Black cultural heritage," making the arts central to their organization and to their vision of the world they sought to create. James Jackson invited Primus to contribute an essay on the "Negro Youth's Heritage in Dance" for one of SNYC's publications. Primus wrote that she was "truly happy to be called on to write the essay."[47]

Given the FBI's ongoing campaigns against black activists and Communists, the Bureau was especially interested in SNYC.

It is therefore not surprising that investigators made note of Primus's involvement with the young radicals. They opened a file on her in September 1944. According to Primus's file, at this time she was also a member of the Communist Party and had been involved in the party since her college years, when she was a member of the Young Communist League, an accusation that she would confirm in later years. If Primus was seen as a great "Negro" dancer by reviewers and other members of the press who hailed her artistry, for the FBI she was "a negress born July 1, 1917[,] at Trinidad, British West Indies."[48] She seems to have first come to their attention when an informant reported that she had been in touch with the Communist Political Association to invite Earl Browder, the general secretary of the Communist Party USA from 1934 to 1945, to her performance.

According to her file, Primus had participated in a number of Communist-sponsored events that encouraged interracial unity and harmony. The Bureau noted her own sponsorship of the Citizens Non-Partisan Committee to Elect Benjamin Davis, the black Communist city councilman from Harlem; her participation in the Negro Freedom Rally, which it referred to as a "monstrous annual affair" run by Communist front organizations; her performances at the Harlem Youth Center and Café Society; and all of the coverage she received in the *Daily Worker*. In this she would have been no different from a number of other prominent artists and intellectuals of the Reformist Left. Like many of these artists, Primus would not have been likely to have had the exposure or critical success that she had without the support of these progressive political and cultural organizations.[49] Many of these organizations were already under surveillance and would become the objects of government investigation during the McCarthy years.

In an interview in the *Daily Worker* in September 1944, Primus spoke "highly of the Southern Negro Congress, with whose leaders she had discussed a plan to include the Arts in their organizing drives," and articulated a philosophy that mirrored the one behind the Double V Campaign. The statement and the context in which it was made helped to make her of interest to the FBI and its director, J. Edgar Hoover. From the distance of time, her perspective doesn't seem that radical. In fact, she appears patriotic, committed to a US victory against fascism, and as fervently devoted to fighting racism at home. Her stance seems little different from that of the civil rights movement then in its infancy, which would soon blossom at the very center of American political life. For the next year, the Bureau sought to find out her naturalization status. But by May 30, 1945, the FBI had lost interest. A note in her file said, "There is no information in the files to indicate that she is either a prominent or influential Communist. Because of her dancing engagements, and theatrical work, it is believed she has very little time for actual Communist activity at present. In view of the fact that she is not considered dangerous to the internal security of the United States at the present time, it is recommended that the Security Index card on Primus be cancelled." The file would be reopened, however, in 1951.[50]

In the FBI affidavit she later gave, Primus said she was led to believe that the best way to aid the Negro in the United States "was through the Communist Party." According to Primus, she joined the party shortly after the Negro Freedom Rally: "My reason for joining the Communist Party, if in fact, I did so, was that I believed that the lot of the Negro in the United States would be best served by the Communist Party." After returning from the South, where she was "appalled" by the conditions of the southern Negro, she resolved to "do whatever possible to help this situation." She went to the *Daily Worker* with suggestions for addressing racial issues more effectively. She wanted to petition the president and Congress, but the receptionist told her that this would be considered treason while the country was still at war. According to Primus, the party's retreat from racial issues during the war years "angered and upset her." In this way she was not unlike the many black activists—or even the fictional protagonist of Ralph Ellison's novel *Invisible Man*, published in the same year of Primus's affidavit. These activists and intellectuals claimed that the Communist Party had abandoned an explicit commitment to the black struggle in favor of supporting the image of a united front between the United States and the Soviet Union in the fight against fascism. They believed that this decision had resulted in the party's unwillingness to be a vocal critic of American racism.

Following her return from the South in 1944, Primus claimed to have suffered a nervous breakdown. Isolated and having received no word or support from her political colleagues, she convalesced at the home of Rockwell Kent at AuSable Forks,

New York. Kent was a painter, printmaker, and writer, and Primus had met him at Café Society. After a brief stay at Kent's home, Primus moved to 536 Madison Street in the Bedford-Stuyvesant section of Brooklyn. While Manhattan would continue to be central to her performance life, she would now call Brooklyn her home. Bedford-Stuyvesant had been a black enclave as early as the nineteenth century, when James Weeks, an African American entrepreneur, began to sell land to other blacks, and some blacks had moved from Harlem to Bedford-Stuyvesant beginning in the 1930s. The area presented the opportunity for home ownership, and many blacks, particularly Caribbean immigrants, chose to relocate there. Madison Street, known for its stately and beautiful brownstones, predominantly housed middle-class blacks. When the A train was constructed in 1936, the New York subway linked the city's two most important black neighborhoods, Harlem and Bed-Stuy.

Upon her recovery, Primus began preparing for her Broadway premier at the Belasco Theater. New York once again provided her with the venue and the audience for her new work. As part of the Belasco program, Primus performed updated versions of "African Ceremonial," "Hard Time Blues," and "Strange Fruit." Her experiences in the South had made her rethink some of her earlier dances. With "Strange Fruit," she would join artists, black and white, who created works that addressed lynching. Talley Beatty premiered "Southern Landscape" in 1947, and Dunham presented "Southland" in 1950. In 1960, Gwendolyn Brooks would write a poem from the perspective of a young white mother who had to continue living with her husband after he brutally murdered a fourteen-year-old black boy named Emmett Till, supposedly for flirting with her. One of the earliest such works, by Paul Laurence Dunbar, a poem called "The Haunted Oak," had appeared in 1903.

Primus's new version of "Strange Fruit" was choreographed as a solo, without music, accompanied only by the spoken words of the Lewis Allan poem. Primus wanted to focus not on the lynched victim or a member of his or her family, but instead on a member of the lynch mob, a woman who had watched the deed. Primus said the character was "not one beloved of the victim, but one of the lynch mob who had been screaming and shouting in animal fury with the rest. Then, the act accomplished and the satisfied mob departed, this one, drained of the poison, stays behind, realizing with grief and terror what has been done."[51]

"Strange Fruit" differed from other Primus performances. Gone were the leaps. In their place, there is a body on the floor, a writhing, distraught human figure, reaching to the tree one moment, fallen down in twists and turns the next. And running but getting nowhere: running in a circle. The isolation of the figure was striking—its profound aloneness, its separateness from both the mob and the lynched body. Its physical isolation seemed to mirror a kind of psychological isolation, a person tormented by her mind, by the lingering horror of what she has witnessed and in which she has participated. There was no transcendence. There was no airy flight. The figure's fixedness to the ground insisted upon a connection between the legacy, the torment and restlessness, of the southern land.

As in "Jim Crow Train," Primus made the lynching scene a canonical moment for her New York audiences. She brought the tragic dimensions of the South to the northern stage in an effort to provoke empathy and action. Like the authors of slave narratives, who often presented sensitive white female characters with whom their northern audiences could identify, Primus made her protagonist a white woman—but one who had both witnessed and taken part in the brutal act. Through works like "Hard Time Blues," "Jim Crow Train," and "Strange Fruit," Primus created a dance narrative of black southern life for New York audiences. This sophisticated group would understand, appreciate, and be moved to political action by her performance.

There is very little footage of Primus dancing in the forties. However, we do have access to eyewitness descriptions and a contemporary restaging that help us appreciate Primus's talent as a dancer and choreographer. In 1945, Donald McKayle, then a high-school senior, saw Primus perform at Central High School of Needle Trades in New York's garment district. McKayle, who attended a different high school, had been invited by his friend Anna, who was an aspiring dancer—and McKayle himself eventually became a dancer. His description is worth quoting at length because it is one of the few first-hand accounts of a Primus concert by someone who was not a critic: "A beautiful vision, a carving in ebony, was dancing. . . . The movements were powerful, yet sparse. It was living sculpture on view. Every curving of her spine, every thrust of her hips, every flapping of her loins, every wave of her heavily

bangled wrists was a gesture from an ancestral ritual of unknown origin." He was especially moved by "Strange Fruit":
"She was a woman consumed with horror, recoiling from a
lynching she had just witnessed," as the words of the poem
were "spoken so beautifully by the actress Vinette Carrol," he
later wrote. The author of the poem "Strange Fruit," Lewis Allan, was actually McKayle's English teacher that year. After
seeing Primus dance—"her feet (running) along the air and
then she landed with the assurance of an avian creature"—
McKayle knew he wanted to be a dancer. He told Anna, "I
want to dance like her!"[52]

Thankfully, a few Primus pieces of the 1940s have been
restaged by contemporary choreographers, including "Strange
Fruit," "The Negro Speaks of Rivers," and "Hard Time Blues."
The choreographer and founder of Urban Bush Women, Jawole Willa Jo Zollar, created a work dedicated to Primus entitled "Walking with Pearl . . . Southern Diaries" inspired by
Primus's trip to the US South and the dances she created based
on that research. The piece includes a restaging of Primus's
"Hard Time Blues" by Kim Bears-Bailey. The quotidian movement of black rural life in the 1940s permeates the movements
of this dance, from the field to the church house, climaxing in
the ecstatic "shout" of the black worshipper. In Zollar's
restaging, a series of dancers take on the part that Primus
danced solo, each expressing the pain, the suffering, the self-
expression, the ecstatic worship and release of the field-
worker. So convincing were the dancers that Zollar has to
remind us of all the technical work, all the rehearsal and

preparation that one must bring to the moment of performance in order to reach a zone where individual stories can be
relayed. For Zollar, dancers are actors, movement actors. "It is
not ritual, but performance," says Zollar. As if to remind viewers
of Primus's skill, Zollar notes that the numerous leaps required of the piece challenge even the best of dancers, requiring the dexterity and strength of "a highly skilled athlete."[53]

When Primus performed "Hard Time Blues" at the Belasco,
she was accompanied by Josh White, who sang the song to guitar accompaniment while she danced. The program also included five male dancers as well as a jazz band and a narrator,
who supplied commentary throughout. In addition to "African
Ceremonial," "Strange Fruit," "Rock Daniel," and "Hard Time
Blues," she also performed "Study in Nothing," set to the music
of her Café Society colleague and friend Mary Lou Williams.
"Slave Market" was a new addition to her repertoire and included two other dancers as well as a number of speakers and
the music of the spirituals. For Broadway, Primus had clearly
staged a more ambitious, theatrical performance, one that
sought to entertain as well as enlighten.

The Belasco was Primus's first Broadway appearance, but it
would not be her last. She helped to choreograph *Show Boat*
for its 1945–1946 season and performed in it as well. After appearing in the Chicago production of *Emperor Jones*, she returned to Broadway in Adolph Thenstead's production of
Caribbean Carnival at the International Theatre in 1947. She
continued to perform throughout the city and began to tour

nationally. With the help of her manager, Austin Wilder, Primus took the "Primus Company," a new dance group she had formed, on a cross-country tour. She also continued to perform at benefits for progressive organizations and causes, which kept her under the watchful eye of the FBI.

Even throughout this busy period, during which she performed both in New York and nationally, Primus also continued to teach at the New Dance Group, helping to develop their offerings in ethnic dance studies. Along with dancers Josephine Premice and Hadassah, she helped to develop a West Indian Dance Program there.

Today, with companies like Alvin Ailey's American Dance Theater, the Dance Theater of Harlem, Philadanco, Urban Bush Women, Ron K. Brown's Evidence, and others, it is difficult to appreciate the dearth of black concert dance in the 1940s and the explosive excitement created by Primus and Katherine Dunham. They approached their work as a mission, a calling, and took it upon themselves to train younger dancers and create opportunities for them.

Performing and teaching also gave Primus the opportunity to perfect her own technique. "The earth is the voice of the dancer. The dancer is the conductor, the wire, which connects the earth and the sky," Primus told her dancers. Movement was marked by variations on the walk: leaping, skipping, hopping, jumping. There were isolated movements of specific body parts: the head, the shoulder, the torso, and the pelvic area. Dancer Jacqueline Hairston danced with Primus in the 1940s and described a typical Primus class. She recalled that the "ballet barre" was essential and that Primus incorporated the methods of Martha Graham, Charles Weidman, and Hanya Holm. She would have students warm up with stretches, bends, and bounces before going to floor exercises, contractions and releases, and isolations of the abdomen, back, legs, and ankles. Then she would work on technique built around three positions of the feet, those signifying a "Ceremonial Pose," "Pride and Elegance," and "Strength and Aggression." These would be followed by the "Earth Series," which focused on the feet in relation to the earth. Next, students would perform excerpts from dances that were already choreographed or those that were works in progress. Primus would close class by telling students the meaning, narrative, and history of one of the dances they had just practiced. An exquisite marriage of her modern dance training and her in-depth research about dance in Africa, Primus's dance classes emphasized that each movement had meaning and each dance had a narrative and a history.[54]

Primus was always an intellectual artist as well as an activist, and her interest in creating her own technique stemmed from this intellectualism. Dance became a way of bearing witness to what her studies revealed, and her activism was driven by a desire to eliminate prejudice, discrimination, and white supremacy. The decision to pursue anthropology at Columbia University was one element in her pursuit of this goal. From 1945 to 1954, Primus took classes toward a PhD. In turning to Columbia, she chose a premier program with a number of pioneering scholars. Her scholarship helped to underscore the significance of African-based cultures, which were still denigrated in the popular imagination. To insist upon the significance of the continent and the cultures that it birthed was a political project in a white supremacist society.

Like Zora Neale Hurston and Katherine Dunham before her, Primus sought to imbue her artistic works with insights that she believed could be garnered from her academic study. In her book recounting the history of modern dance, *Modern Bodies*, Julia L. Foulkes noted that for black women such as Dunham, Primus, and dancer/choreographer Syvilla Fort, higher education helped to legitimate artistic pursuits. Anthropology was a field that attracted a number of women and minorities because it called for serious scientific investigation of all forms of culture and society, including those not yet deemed worthy of study by disciplines such as history or literature. Primus noted, in an interview, "With anthropology I could gain the facts about which I danced—the facts and not just the feelings."[55]

Primus's intellectual pursuits were driven by an activist motivation, not just an artistic one. Along with Hurston and Dunham, she adhered to a school of thought furthered by Franz Boas and Melville Herskovits, who countered claims that African Americans had lost any sense of connection to Africa. For them, Africa could be found in every element of diasporic cultures, from religious practices and foodways to music and dance. So, although Primus did not work with Boas or Herskovits, her work contributed to their broader project of situating Africa as central to the development of New World cultures.

At the beginning of her academic career at Columbia, Primus took classes such as "Primitive Languages," "Cultural Dynamics," "Peoples and Cultures of Africa," "Native Cultures of South America," "Primitive Art and Its Contribution to Modern Art," and "Art of the Congo." One is struck by the liberal use of the word "primitive" even in this most progressive department. In 1946, she took a course entitled "Religions of Primitive Peoples" with Ruth Benedict. The course was "a survey of the religious beliefs and religious techniques with special emphasis on religion in relation to the social order." Benedict, a pioneering anthropologist, a student of Franz Boas, and a peer of Margaret Mead, championed the importance of acknowledging the value of cultures based on their own contexts. Benedict was the author of two major studies, *The Chrysanthemum and the Sword*, on Japan, and *Patterns of Culture*, an introduction to cultural studies. She also coauthored, with colleague Gene Weltfish, an instructor with whom Primus also studied, a World War II–era pamphlet entitled "Races of Mankind." Meant for servicemen, the pamphlet provided scientific arguments against racism. In short, Primus was taught by antiracist intellectuals whose scholarship demonstrated how scholarly work might inform a project of social change.

Primus did not finish her doctorate at Columbia. She would do so many years later at another of the city's prominent educational institutions, New York University. However, Columbia was an important site of her intellectual development, and the Columbia Department of Anthropology provided her with some of the tools she needed to pursue her interest in the significance and centrality of dance. While attending classes, Primus continued to perform, and she further honed her teaching skills and her educational presentations about dance.

In 1945, under the auspices of the New Dance Group, Primus conducted a series of lectures and demonstrations on the influence of African dance on dance in Haiti and the American South. She was clearly establishing herself as both a performer and an intellectual. Articulate, intelligent, well educated, and well read, she was not only capable of executing sophisticated movement, but also had the chops to analyze and talk about what she performed. She had always aspired to be an educator, and her time at Columbia gave her the set of concepts she needed to convey the meaning and significance of her dancing. Dance, which provided access to a people's culture and their struggle, was a perfect mechanism for teaching her audiences about their roots. The dancer could walk in their footsteps and express their longings. Given her commitment to education, it is not surprising that Primus embarked on a college tour.

During her company's tour of black colleges, Primus performed at Fisk University in 1948. Dr. Edward Embree, president of the Julius Rosenwald Fund, was in the audience. Convinced of the authenticity of her company's performance, Dr. Embree asked Primus when she had last visited Africa. "I've never been," Primus replied. Embree arranged for Primus to receive a $4,000 grant, the foundation's last and largest research grant. The Rosenwald Fund had provided support for both Zora Neale Hurston and Katherine Dunham to conduct their own anthropological studies.

The Caribbean, especially Trinidad, and the American South had been Primus's gateway to the traditions of Africa, but now she would have an opportunity to experience Africa firsthand. Armed with a gun, DDT, inoculations, and her studies in anthropological method, Primus left for her trip in December 1948. Obviously, she thought she would encounter bugs, disease, and violence. Instead, she acquired so much more. While there she traveled to the Gold Coast, Nigeria, Angola, Cameroon, Ivory Coast, Liberia, French Equatorial Africa, and the Belgian Congo. She performed, learned from traditional dancers, and participated in spontaneous community dances. According to Primus, village elders throughout Africa believed the ancestors had taught her. In Nigeria, she was given the name Omowale, which meant "Child returned home." Upon her return to the United States, she would become one of African dance's major ambassadors, introducing generations of dancers and audiences to the dynamism, beauty, and history of African dance.

When Primus came back to the United States in 1950, she found a political climate that was vastly different from the one she had left when embarking on her African sojourn. Many of her colleagues and peers were under investigation, and the institutions that had nurtured her were challenged. She would continue to be the object of investigation and surveillance—an experience she shared with a number of her colleagues and collaborators. The FBI opened a file on Josephson in 1943 and placed him on the Security Index in 1944. From then on, he was under constant surveillance. By 1950 his passport was confiscated. J. Edgar Hoover and the powerful columnist Walter Winchell were architects of Café Society's demise. Fittingly, the two often met at the tony Stork Club, the venue Café Society parodied. Eventually a number of people associated with the club would be blacklisted or required to appear before the House Un-American Activities Committee (HUAC). Zero Mostel, Paul Robeson, Canada Lee, Lewis Allan, Lillian Helman, Hazel Scott, Josh White, and Lena Horne were all called before the committee. In their appearances, Scott and White blamed their involvement with the Communist Left on Josephson.

Josephson later fell out with Primus because he emphatically believed she named names during the McCarthy era. Himself the victim of Senator Joseph McCarthy's witch-hunt, he could never forgive her for having done so. He claimed that she told the press, "I don't know why they're doing this to me. I was an informer for the FBI all those years I was dancing at Café Society." In his memoir, Josephson insisted that Primus was an informer even before this time, while she was working for the Maritime Union. There is no evidence for Josephson's claims, even in Primus's FBI file. Primus almost certainly never named names—though she did admit to her own attraction to and involvement with the Communist Party as well as her support of and sympathy for Communist causes during this period. Josephson went from being reluctant to hire her because of her appearance, to becoming an employer who supported her career, to becoming a former political ally who held her in contempt. He grew to resent her, believing that she had used him to establish her career and then left his club when other opportunities arose.[56]

Though he was probably wrong about her naming names, Josephson may have been correct in noting Primus's ambition. Primus always recognized opportunities for advancement and seized them; where they did not exist, she created them. Many progressive people believed that appearing before the FBI or the House Un-American Activities Committee in and of itself legitimated their activities. Josephson would not have been alone in feeling betrayed by Primus, Josh White, and Hazel Scott, all of whom voluntarily met with government agencies during the anti-Communist hysteria.

By that time, Primus had traveled extensively through Africa, the Middle East, and Europe. The FBI took her passport upon her return, thereby limiting her research, performance opportunities, and income. In this way her experience was like that of W. E. B. Du Bois and Paul Robeson. Through her lawyer, Herbert Mont Levy of the American Civil Liberties Union, Primus set up an interview with the FBI offices in New York on October 2, 1952, for the sole purpose of obtaining her passport, with a follow-up meeting on October 16. There she provided letters and documents from numerous organizations said to have been Communist fronts. In a memo dated November 3, 1952, an FBI agent wrote: "In as much as the signed statement furnished by Miss Primus reflects that she is not presently connected with the Communist Party, no attempt will be made by the NYO to develop her as an informant. It is not believed that further investigation in this matter is warranted." Another

memo, dated November 21 (see Appendix A), is important because in spite of Josephson's assertion to the contrary, it
strongly suggests that she did not name names.[57]

In addition to finding a Left decimated by the federal government, Primus would also find a black movement that
would compromise the goal of economic justice in order to
make gains in domestic civil rights. The movement seemed
to eschew the international dimensions of its calls for anti-
colonial, racial equality.

In spite of this new political landscape, Primus continued to
work to bring African culture to the international concert
stage, and in so doing, she gained many admirers. She inspired poems, essays, and paintings. She continued to share
her knowledge in the dance studio, in the lecture hall, and on
the college campus. Along the way, she documented, analyzed,
and theorized about the role of dance in human development.
She inspired new generations of dancers and choreographers,
from Alvin Ailey to Bill T. Jones to Jawole Willa Jo Zollar, all of
whom paid tribute to her in their own choreography. By the
time of her death in 1994, Pearl Primus was widely recognized
as one of the foremothers of black concert dance.

In New York during the 1940s, Pearl Primus created a dance
narrative that highlighted the struggle against segregation and
racial violence. As such she made the plight of black Americans, particularly black southerners, a central concern in the
fight for American democracy.

Seventeen years after Pearl Primus's death, the novelist
Sapphire created a fictional character, Toosie Johnston, who
saw Primus dance in the 1940s. Through Toosie, Sapphire

gives voice to those migrants who sat in Primus's audience when she danced "Jim Crow Car," "Hard Time Blues," and "Strange Fruit":

> One night Pearl Primus herse'f, yes indeedy. Dat woman jumped five feet in de air if she jumped a inch! Den she did a dance to some country blues near 'bout tear my heart out watchin' it. Made me think of de plantation, all what I escaped from, runned away from. Even all I been through, I still think it good I left. Josh White record playing while she dancin'. Everybody sittin' dere knowed what she was talkin' 'bout or was holdin' on to somebody dat knew."[58]

Sapphire's fictional migrant captures the excitement of those who witnessed Pearl Primus's choreographed flights. Her journeys through time and space spoke to their yearning and motivated their drive to change the nation and the world.

CHAPTER TWO

ANN PETRY: WALKING HARLEM

While Pearl Primus was bringing the plight of black southerners to the New York stage, Ann Petry was addressing the concerns of black urbanites, especially the inhabitants of Harlem, in her writing. Primus danced in venues throughout New York; Petry spent most of her time uptown, where she lived and worked from 1938 until the mid-1940s. Harlem provided Petry with ample material and inspiration, and she created a body of work that earned her an international literary reputation.

Petry used fiction to map Harlem, both as a *space* constructed by forces outside of its control and as a *place* created by its inhabitants. The two were necessarily at odds with each other. While Harlem the place fought against racism, the space existed as a black neighborhood because of forced residential segregation. It grew into a global black cultural and political capital because of the creativity and determination of those who

Portrait of Ann Petry. Photo by Edna Guy.

lived there. In Petry's fiction, the space is plagued by substandard housing; the place was filled with individuals trying desperately to create meaningful lives for themselves and their children. Like the characters about whom she wrote, Petry walked the streets of Harlem. She navigated them as an activist, journalist, and writer of fiction. These combined roles informed her work, ensuring that her writing possessed a sense of urgency, realism, and artistry. The Harlem she documented changed constantly; it was made and remade by walkers, who in turn were shaped by the streets they walked.

When *The Crisis* published her short story "On Saturday the Siren Sounds at Noon" in its December 1943 issue, Petry quickly emerged as an important up-and-coming writer. All the elements that would characterize her later work can be identified in this riveting tale. The tensely woven story, only two pages long, was based on a newspaper article about two children who met their deaths in an apartment fire while their parents were at work. Petry focused on the children's father, who, in a series of flashbacks sparked by an air-raid siren, recalls the day he found his burned children. Petry tweaked the facts as she transformed the account into fiction. In her version, the children are left home alone by the man's adulterous wife. The story brought her to the attention of an editor at Houghton Mifflin in Boston, who encouraged her to write a novel. In 1945, she received a Houghton Mifflin Literary Fellowship so she could complete that novel, *The Street*.

A native of Old Saybrook, Connecticut, Ann Petry was the descendant of four generations of African American New Englanders. Born on October 12, 1908,[1] Anna Houston Lane was the second daughter of Peter Clark Lane and Bertha James Lane. The Lanes were one of fifteen black families who lived in Old Saybrook, a small town located where the Connecticut River meets the Long Island Sound. Petry's father owned the local drugstore and worked as a pharmacist; her mother was a licensed chiropodist—one who treats corns and bunions. Imbued with an entrepreneurial spirit, Mrs. Lane also worked as a beautician and barber and was the owner of Fine Linens for Fine Homes, a business that employed a number of Irish immigrant women as makers of handmade linen and lace tablecloths and napkins. As such, the Lanes were solidly middle class—in status if not always financially.

A bookish, chubby child, Petry lost herself in reading and from a young age aspired to be a writer. Her family had other plans for her. Upon graduating from Old Saybrook High School, she first enrolled in the historic Hampton Normal and Agricultural Institute in Virginia, where other members of her family had gone. Petry's aunts and uncles who had attended Hampton were adventurers, college administrators, and successful professionals. One of her aunts, Anna Louise James, was a licensed pharmacist. Petry's own aspirations were more intellectual and artistic than business oriented, so she felt Hampton was not a good fit. She attended Hampton for a year and a half before returning to Connecticut. She never went back to the school and never spoke publicly about her time there. According to her daughter, Elisabeth, Petry was "dissatisfied with her courses in meal preparation and management of household expenses" and wanted to learn about more than the domestic sciences.[2] Booker T. Washington had also attended Hampton, acquiring his philosophy of industrial education there. Building upon this foundation, Washington later developed a disavowal of protest politics. Hampton became the model for Washington's Tuskegee Institute in Tuskegee, Alabama.

Unlike Washington, Petry actively engaged in protests at Hampton. It appears that she may have even been involved in a student strike. After her death, Elisabeth discovered a copy of student demands insisting that "teachers needed 'apparent education' above that of the students and that the teachers in the trade school should possess at least a high school diploma."[3] Eventually, Petry transferred to the University of Connecticut, where she earned a degree from the College of Pharmacy in 1931. Following in the footsteps of her father and her beloved aunt, Anna Louise, who had been the first black woman to receive a degree in pharmacy, Petry worked for a number of years in the family's Old Saybrook store before managing their other property in Old Lyme.

Petry seemed to resent her parents' decision to send her to Hampton and to pharmaceutical college. Her older sister, Bertha, had been sent to Pembroke (Brown University's sister school), but the Lanes' ambitions for their younger daughter seemed decidedly different from those they'd had for their elder daughter. When Petry transferred to the University of Connecticut, she encountered daughters of the black elite who, according to Elisabeth Petry, "were being groomed for race leadership." One friend, Jane Bolin, was the daughter of the first black graduate of Williams College and went on to become the first black woman judge in New York State. While Petry met lifelong friends at the University of Connecticut, she nonetheless felt very insecure about her prospects. In a journal entry from 1945, she wrote, "In comparison to all these people I was fat, with no perceptible waistline, had no clothes, no money, no boy friends—and of course all the other social figures were slender, extremely well-dressed, knew how to giggle and be coy and were well-supplied with funds."[4]

Petry felt like an outsider when she was among the daughters of the black bourgeoisie, although, given her own family's businesses and educational pedigree, she was not entirely out of her league in terms of status. Though not wealthy, the Lanes were an important black New England family; they were property owners who had been freeborn for generations before the end of slavery. She also grew to be a very attractive woman. Later, her ability to gain entry into black bourgeois circles would prove to be most helpful as she wrote her weekly "Lighter Side" society column for the Harlem-based newspaper, the *People's Voice*. Significantly, though, the black bourgeoisie would not become the subject of Petry's fiction. Perhaps it was because she felt like an outsider and never completely identified with the social world of the black elite. She was always drawn to novels that portrayed social problems, such as those of Émile Zola, Charles Dickens, and Theodore Dreiser, and she began to publish in an era when there was a readership for just this kind of fiction. The critical and commercial success of Richard Wright's *Native Son* (1940) proved there was an audience for socially conscious, realist narratives by black writers. Petry was one of a number of young black writers who began to publish novels in the wake of Wright's success.

Possessed of a strong sense of intellectual and artistic ambition, Petry ultimately decided to pursue her own path in spite of family objections. At home, when she was not working in the pharmacy, she read widely and deeply. She read books by nineteenth-century French, British, and Russian novelists. She read in psychology and economics. Eventually, she tried her hand at writing. Feeling terribly stifled and fearing she would never fully pursue her artistic ambitions in Connecticut, Petry soon set her sights on New York. She began making frequent trips to the city to attend the theater and visit the New York Public Library. As early as March 21, 1936, the *Amsterdam News* ran a small story entitled "Connecticut Druggist Likes Shows, So She Comes Here." The piece that followed explained that the daughter of a prominent Saybrook family came to see Broadway shows; when in New York, she stayed at the Emma Ransom House, a women's residence at the Harlem YWCA named for an early-twentieth-century black activist. Among the small, close-knit black elite of the time, Petry's family was prominent enough for her comings and goings to be noteworthy.[5]

New York had other attractions as well. George David Petry was born in New Iberia, Louisiana, but had been sent to New York by his father for high school, since there were few schools in Louisiana that would allow black students to attend.[6] He and Ann (she dropped the final "a" from her name) met at the home of a mutual friend in Hartford, Connecticut. George was an aspiring writer also. Soon after they met, and unbeknownst to Ann's family, they secretly married in a March 13, 1936, ceremony in Mount Vernon, New York; nearly two years later, on February 22, 1938, the couple held a small, elegant ceremony at her family's Old Saybrook home. Even the first date would have made Petry significantly older than most first-time brides of the period. Already, it seems, she had decided to follow a path quite different from that of her peers.

New York was exhilarating for Petry. After officially relocating to New York in 1938, she and George moved to 2 East 129th Street, just on the corner of Fifth Avenue. In New York, Petry left the pharmacy behind. She first found employment selling advertising and writing ad copy for a wig company; then transitioned to journalism, reporting for the *People's Voice*. Soon her schedule was full of cultural activity, reporting, and volunteer work, particularly for children's and black civic organizations. All would provide material for her fiction.

Petry also found time to enjoy Harlem's nightlife. An avid fan of jazz, she attended some of the area's legendary clubs to listen to the music. She met the composer Frances Kraft Reckling, and the two women became lifelong friends. Reckling studied at the Boston Conservatory of Music, arranged a number of songs for big bands, wrote popular and gospel songs, and taught piano. She also owned Reckling's Music Store, which was on the same floor as the *People's Voice* offices. Reckling held book parties and other events at her store. Years later,

Petry seemed stunned by a photograph from one of her own book signings. In a journal entry on August 4, 1982, she wrote: "Frances Reckling sent me a batch of old photographs to look at . . . of Langston Hughes—one of me with Langston and a man I do not remember ever having seen before . . . at a reception at Frances' store—evidently *Country Place* had just been published—me with orchid, holding a coffee cup & cigarette. All of us smiling."[7] If indeed the reception was for her novel *Country Place*, then the event would have occurred sometime in 1947, before Petry left New York for Connecticut, but after she and George moved to the Bronx. The photograph reminded her of her days as a sophisticated urbanite, one of the New York literati. Reckling would always be associated with this image of herself, one who led the exciting, artistically intense cultural life of a young New Yorker.

During her first few months in Harlem, Petry began another friendship that would prove to be influential for her. She met Dollie Robinson, a committed trade unionist and political activist, in 1938, after Petry had written a story about a union for the *People's Voice*. They would go on to help cofound Negro Women Incorporated, a consumers rights group that was also the women's auxiliary of Adam Clayton Powell Jr.'s People's Committee. The People's Committee mobilized Harlemites to protest and picket against a number of issues facing their community. Elisabeth Petry recalled that her mother considered Robinson "one of her guardian angels when Daddy was in the army."[8] Petry drew inspiration from both Robinson and Reckling for her fiction. Members of Robinson's family became the basis for characters in Petry's third novel, *The Narrows*, and Reckling might be credited with the prominent place of music in her first, *The Street*. In fact, Lutie Johnson, the protagonist of *The Street*, sings Reckling's "Darlin'" while sitting at the bar of a neighborhood club. While Petry and Reckling shared an interest in music, Petry and Robinson bonded over their activist commitments.

On July 3, 1943, Petry's life changed dramatically when George was inducted into the US Army. He entered active service on July 24 at Camp Upton, New York, and remained in the military until his discharge on October 4, 1946, at Camp Pickett, Virginia. Many years later, George Petry still recalled his anger at his country for treating German POWs better than black GI's. But one memory in particular continued to sting. He often told his daughter and others the story of his having been asked, by a priest, to leave a Roman Catholic Church in the nation's capital. He was given a list of churches where he would "feel more comfortable." According to Elisabeth Petry, her father "never went back to church except to attend the odd wedding."[9]

George's treatment as a black man in uniform was not lost on Petry. Indeed, black soldiers and their experiences in a Jim Crow military found their way into much of her fiction. She was not alone in her concern with the "Negro soldier," either. Much of black America expressed pride in their boys in uniform, but at the same time, they were furious at their treatment by their fellow soldiers, other citizens, and their nation. Consequently, the armed forces became a primary focus of the black press and black activism during the war years. The military was well aware of this perception. In 1944, the army created the propaganda documentary *The Negro Soldier*, directed by Frank Capra as part of his morale-boosting series Why We Fight. The film countered the racist stereotypes that still prevailed in Hollywood. Instead of showing blacks as cowardly servants and minstrels, it narrated a history of dignified and dedicated individuals who contributed to US military history. In reality, black enlisted men were still relegated to menial roles and subjected to harassment and worse. However, on the streets of Harlem and in other black neighborhoods, they were treated as heroes.

In her fiction, Petry portrayed a Harlem that sent its sons off to a Jim Crow military and left its daughters to fend for themselves in a world that saw them as easy prey. She also portrayed the Harlem of those who remained behind: the working poor, the southern migrants. Though more often than not, Petry saw the contradictions in the promise of American democracy and the American Dream, she nonetheless maintained a belief in her nation's ability to change. Like other activists of her generation, she strove to "achieve" her country's possibilities by working to consistently point out these contradictions, particularly with regard to race, but with regard to class and gender as well. She sought to remedy those problems by working with political organizations as well as within local government. Through her fiction, she sought, time and again, to demonstrate the high social costs of the most fundamental paradox of American democracy: its treatment of its black citizens. This perspective is one she may have inherited from over a century of black thought, but it was crystallized during her Harlem years, the years that inspired her most prolific period.

Petry worked closely with Communists and would later defend them. She believed they were equally devoted to resolving the contradictions of the American Dream. But, unlike Primus, Petry was never a member of the Communist Party. In fact, like a number of African Americans of earlier generations, Petry was a lifelong Republican. However, with the exception of Dwight D. Eisenhower, she voted for Democratic presidential candidates. She was active on the Old Saybrook Republican Town Committee and served on Saybrook's Board of Education as a Republican. For a number of blacks, the Republicans were the party of Lincoln, and, like many of them, Petry could not reconcile herself to the presence of "Dixiecrats," southern Democrats who supported segregation, in the Democratic Party.

So, let's take a walk with Ann Petry through Harlem, circa the early 1940s—anytime before the Harlem Riot of August 1, 1943. If it is a weekday we might head to the offices of the *People's Voice*, where Petry served as the "women's editor" from 1941 to 1944. The *People's Voice* offices were located at 210 West 125th, on top of Woolworth's and across the street from the Apollo Theater, right in the heart of Harlem. As we walk west on 125th, past Lenox to Eighth, we see soldiers in their khakis and a sailor or two. Women walk swiftly, with a sense of urgency and purpose, hats on, purses held tightly, wearing round-toe heels and pumps. A group of men linger outside a record store, flirting with the young women who walk by them. There's a particularly flirty young beauty dressed in the tightest of skirts, curls piled atop her head; she looks a little like the delightful Hazel Scott about the eyes.[10]

At the *People's Voice*, Petry not only worked as the women's editor but also had a weekly column, the "Lighter Side," documenting the activities of Harlem's elite. In addition, she wrote feature news stories and occasional profiles of civic leaders and celebrities, including an interview with the green-eyed Fredi Washington, one of black America's first movie stars and sister-in-law of the *Voice's* illustrious publisher, Adam Clayton Powell Jr. He would eventually divorce Washington's sister Isabel to marry Hazel Scott in 1945.

Along with the *Amsterdam News* and the *New York Age*, the *People's Voice* was the newest of Harlem's three weeklies. Powell, an activist, preacher, and politician, the pastor of the Abyssinian Baptist Church, and a New York City councilman, had founded the *Voice* in 1942. The paper ran from February 14, 1942, to April 24, 1948. Powell referred to it as "the Lenox Ave. edition of the *Daily Worker*." As part of the vast network of black newspapers, the *People's Voice* joined others in the black press as they insisted upon the eradication of segregation in housing, access to education and wartime jobs, an end to lynching, and, most importantly, the desegregation of the armed services. One government report found that although most blacks in New York listened to the same radio stations and read the same newspapers as whites, especially the *New York Daily News*, the black press had a tremendous impact on black public opinion. According to the report, "the overwhelming majority of blacks—more than eight out of ten—

read some black newspaper, usually either the *Amsterdam News* or the *People's Voice*."[11]

In fact, the government was especially interested in the black press during World War II because of its vocal critique of American racism and its commitment to Double V. Such criticism of American society and government was seen as potentially subversive to the war effort. A number of newspapers were under investigation; J. Edgar Hoover felt that the Roosevelt administration should use wartime sedition powers to indict members of the black press. While there were no indictments, black newspapers were encouraged to tone down their critiques of racism and racial segregation. The *People's Voice* was a special concern for Hoover. He observed that although the paper claimed to support the war effort and the administration, it nonetheless published articles that he felt "contributed to the breach and extreme feeling between white and colored races." Hoover was expressly troubled about an editorial cartoon depicting a black soldier who represented 450,000 black servicemen. There were chains on his wrists to dramatize the way blacks were kept from combat. The paper was also considered pro-Communist because of the tone of its editorials and the presence of Communists on its staff.[12]

Without question, the *Voice* was the most radical of the Harlem papers. Upon its founding, Powell, whose political campaigns had been supported by progressives, liberals, and members of the Communist Party, immediately hired a number of important black Communist intellectuals. By the end of the decade, he would fire all of them as part of a Communist

People's Voice newsroom, c. 1942. The woman on the far left is believed to be Ann Petry. Photo by Morgan Smith.

purge encouraged by the growing influence of Senator Joseph McCarthy, and by what Powell saw as a threat to his own political ambition. But initially, the paper's editorial leadership was largely Communist. It included Executive Editor Doxey Wilkerson (who later left to become editor of the *New York Daily Worker*), reporter Max Yergan, and the "de facto" managing editor, Marvel Cooke. Civil rights and union activist Wilkerson worked for Roosevelt's Advisory Committee on Education and was also a columnist for the *Daily Worker*. He served on the national committee of the Communist Party, but resigned in 1957 following revelations about Stalin's atrocities, which shook much of the American Left and undermined their commitment to the party.[13] Activist and journalist Marvel Cooke was the first woman journalist at the *Amsterdam News* and the first African American or woman reporter at the white *Daily Compass*. Her well-regarded investigative piece "I Was a Slave" was published in the *Compass* in 1950. It focused on the exploitation of black domestic workers at the Bronx Slave Market, the name given to the corner where white women hired black domestic workers to clean their homes for the day. Max Yergan was a highly regarded leftist activist who served as president of the National Negro Congress, a coalition of African American labor, religious, and fraternal organizations.

The leftist politics of the paper's leadership is evident in an early editorial announcing the paper's mission: "We are men and women of the people. The people are ours and we are theirs. . . . THIS IS A WORKING CLASS PAPER." The editorial went on to pledge support for the trade union movement and to fight for lower rent, better housing, and equal access to health facilities and schools. Finally, the editors asserted: "We are against Hitlerism abroad and just as strongly against Hitlerism at home." This statement linked the paper to the larger Double V Campaign, though the editors were concerned with a much broader platform than Double V, which was largely focused on segregation in the military.[14]

The *People's Voice* editorial gives insight into Petry's own politics, which were clearly informed by the heady radicalism of her work and extracurricular environments. Her reporting, writing, and activism focused on many of the issues taken up by the newspaper: housing, segregation, equal opportunity, and the fight against white supremacy at home and abroad. Petry's challenge would be to translate this political stance into a set of aesthetic principles; she did so by situating working-class protagonists at the center of her fiction, creating a language that expressed the urgency and tension of Harlem streets, and demonstrating the psychological complexity of the urban poor. Her own political and aesthetic interests would lead her to focus on gender as much as she did on class and race.

As women's editor, features writer, and columnist, Petry was involved in every aspect of the newspaper and worked very closely with other editors in shaping the paper's editorial policy. Her coworkers included the political cartoonist Ollie Harrington and the photographer Morgan Smith—who, with his twin brother, Marvin, chronicled Harlem's residents, newsmakers, artists, entertainers, leaders, and athletes. Like those of Smith and Harrington, Petry's aesthetic approach and political opinions are evident in her work at the *People's Voice*. They were shaped by what she observed and experienced in Harlem. While at the *People's Voice*, she reported on events held by the Harlem elite. The ladies of her "Lighter Side" columns might have been the daughters of the women depicted in the novels of her Harlem Renaissance predecessors Nella Larsen and Jessie Fauset: they were light-skinned, civic-minded clubwomen, often the glamorous wives of Harlem's businessmen, politicians, and entertainers. But she also wrote an open letter to New York City mayor Fiorello LaGuardia in May 1943 requesting that he reopen the Savoy Ballroom, which had been closed in the spring of 1943 as a "base for vice." LaGuardia claimed that 164

servicemen who had met women there had contracted vene-
real disease. Walter White of the NAACP argued that if this
was the case, then the Waldorf Astoria should have been closed
as well. Many, including Powell, insisted that the real reason for
closing the Savoy was "race mixing." Petry asserted in her letter
that the Savoy was not only an important site of entertainment
for Harlemites and other New Yorkers, but also "a place for
civic organizations like the NAACP and the National Urban
League [to hold] events that benefit the community."[15]

Petry also petitioned for funding for the Harlem Arts Center
as an important place for after-school programs for children.
She covered the activities of the many organizations in which
she was involved, announcing soirees, fundraisers, and public
events in the *Voice*. She wrote feature-length stories on the federal government's warnings to white GI's about Harlem's black
prostitutes, including responses from some of Harlem's women.
Another feature focused on the trial of three Puerto Rican
youths charged with murdering a white man who had solicited
prostitutes in their neighborhood.

The relationship between racist stereotypes of black
women's sexuality and the public policies and practices that resulted from them also informed Petry's fiction, especially her
best-selling novel *The Street*. The novel's protagonist, Lutie
Johnson, is constantly assaulted with opinions about and ex-
pectations of her sexuality simply because she is a black woman.
While working as a domestic in Connecticut, Lutie is frequently insulted by her employer's friends, white women who
insist that black servants are sexually promiscuous. In New

York she is often offered money or other favors in exchange for sex. Ultimately, she is the victim of sexual harassment by both black and white men—and two attempted rapes. The vulnerability of black women to sexual abuse and exploitation is a recurrent theme in the novel.

Petry's interest in the children of working-class mothers is evident in both her activism and her fiction. During this time, she also worked for the Laundry Workers Joint Board, preparing programs for the children of laundry workers, and in 1943 she joined Harlem's Play Schools Association Project at Public School No. 10 as a recreation specialist. Petry helped to develop a program for the children of working parents at the school, which was located at St. Nicholas Avenue and 116th Street. She was acutely aware of "latchkey" children, who appeared in Harlem long before they became evident nationwide. While Petry's work and activism sought to provide safe space for these children during the hours between the end of school and the end of their parents' workday, her fiction demonstrated the perils, such as gangs and exploitive adults, that awaited them on the streets of Harlem when such programs were insufficient.[16]

In her fiction, then, Petry sought to give a fuller, more complex picture of the social problems she encountered as a reporter; in her activism, she sought to address these problems through organizing. It's not surprising that her journalism reported both the issues and the efforts to address them. Her fiction elaborates upon the human cost and resulting frustration, but it rarely gives life to activists' efforts. In an interview with the *Daily Worker*, Petry noted, "I feel that the portrayal of a problem in itself, in all its cruelty and horror, is actually the thing which sets people thinking, and not any solution that may be offered in a novel."[17]

Still on our tour of Harlem's streets to see what Petry saw, we might accompany her, after leaving the offices of the *People's Voice*, to any number of civic or artistic meetings or events. If the Harlem Riverside Defense Council, where Petry was assistant to the secretary, was not meeting, we would attend a meeting of the National Association of Colored Graduate Nurses, where Petry served as publicity director. She was in the thick of the association's efforts to become part of the National Association of Graduate Nurses and to integrate the wartime nurses corps.

The war provided African Americans a perfect opportunity to challenge every aspect of segregation. Jim Crow laws and practices were seen as the primary challenge to American democracy, especially during the war years, when America's claims to freedom and equality were in the spotlight. Because black people had been barred from professional organizations such as the American Medical Association and the American Bar Association, they founded their own, the National Medical Association and the Negro Bar Association. The National Association of Colored Graduate Nurses was founded in 1908 in response to the exclusion of black women from white professional associations and their lack of access to education and state licensing. In 1948, the American Nurses Association (ANA) became integrated. Unfortunately, black women still found themselves denied leadership positions in the ANA, and their contributions were rarely recognized. In 1971, during another period of heightened militancy, black nurses founded the National Black Nurses Association. But in the early 1940s, black professionals were still dedicated to the fight to integrate American society. Petry, like others of her generation, was never a separatist; she believed in and fought for integration.[18]

While still actively involved in civic organizations, Petry soon began to devote most of her time and energy to a new organization that she helped to found with Dollie Robinson: Negro Women Incorporated. In fact, the organizing meeting was held in the offices of the *People's Voice*. The organization seems to have been the outgrowth of an earlier effort, the Harlem Housewives League, for which Petry served in a number of administrative capacities. The newer, more militant group was, according to its founding document, "a Harlem consumer's watch group that provide[d] working class women with 'how-to' information for purchasing food, clothing, and furniture." In fact, the organization sought to do much more than provide women with information. Other founding documents noted that it would "organize women for mass participation in the war effort." One event, "Negro Women Have a Vote—How Shall They Use It?" was an effort to encourage black women to recognize themselves as political agents. The speakers included prominent black women liberals and leftists, including Communist journalist Marvel Cooke, Civil Rights Congress leader Ada B. Jackson, and the Communist city councilman, Ben Davis Jr.[19]

An invitation to the Negro Women Incorporated's first meeting appeared in the May 2, 1942, edition of the *People's Voice*:

> War economy upsets and dislocates everything. First Aid, Nutrition—[we want] a community alert, consumer information centers, [we] believe in fighting for the rights of Negro women, Fighting rising food cost, disseminat[ing] info on women's organizing in Harlem. Deluge LaGuardia with postcards and letters protesting the end of children's art classes at the Harlem Art Center. IF YOU ARE INTERESTED IN YOURSELF AS A WOMAN, IN HARLEM AS A PLACE TO LIVE DURING AND AFTER THE WAR IS OVER, COME TO THE FIRST MEETING. LET'S GO PLACES!

What is striking about this invitation is that it was a call to build a movement and was filled with language demanding active, forward-moving momentum. The invitation acknowledged that the war economy had left women—many of whom were fighting these battles alone while their husbands were fighting overseas—with a sense of flux, of chaos. But in chaos is possibility, the invitation intimated, and chaotic energies organized can generate constructive movement, action: "Deluge" LaGuardia, "protest," "fight"—and the final call, which could serve as the mantra of black America at this time—"Let's Go Places!" Thousands of blacks were migrating from the South and the Caribbean into Los Angeles, Detroit, Chicago, Philadelphia, and New York for wartime jobs; hundreds of thousands were serving as soldiers overseas; and untold numbers were willing to march and protest segregation at home, even threatening to march on Washington. The invitation captured a sense of movement, action, confidence, and political optimism, for agents of change were finally on the move. It was the same spirit that was embodied by campaigns like the "Don't Buy Where You Can't Work" protests led by Adam Clayton Powell Jr. Through these efforts, Harlem streets were stages for political theater; street-corner speeches, protest marchers, and rallies all energized the neighborhood.

Nonetheless, Petry was acutely aware that large numbers of black people had not yet been swept up in this sense of possibility. For them, the changes and the pace of the movement only brought a sense of overwhelming disruption. If her journalism focused on the movement, on the possibility, if her civic and political work tried to organize this energy, her fiction focused on those ordinary Harlemites whose lives escaped the containing narratives of organized protest. The people of her fiction are mobile, walking in crowds and riding on buses, subways, suburban commuter trains. The pace of her fiction is fast, and yet there is no sense that her urban characters ever transcend the limitations placed upon them and "arrive."

Petry's emerging ideas about her art were not informed by her journalism and her activism alone. She also found herself becoming part of a community of activist-oriented artists. Some evenings she jumped on the subway or walked up to the New York Public Library at 135th Street, where the American Negro Theater (ANT) rehearsed. Petry joined this troupe shortly after Abraham Hill and Frederick O'Neal founded it in

1940. For one year she performed as Tillie Petunia in Hill's *On Strivers Row*, a social farce set in Harlem and centered around the debut of a young socialite, Cobina. The role of Cobina was played by a young, aspiring actress named Ruby Dee. As Tillie Petunia, Petry was a hypocritical, class-conscious gossip columnist. Dee eventually earned fame for her role in the 1961 film *A Raisin in the Sun*. In 1980, she and her husband, Ossie Davis, would produce a series of programs for PBS, one of which was based on Petry's early short story "Solo on the Drums." Hill and O'Neal sought to create a community-based theater that would present plays about black life. Of her American Negro Theater experience, Petry would later write: "We put 'On Strivers Row' on three nights a week. And there were a lot of famous people who had their start, you know, in that theater . . . Ruby Dee, Ossie Davis, Harry Belafonte." Like Petry's fiction, *On Strivers Row* focused on Harlem's growing class divide, though it centered on the elite even as it critiqued them. Petry would focus on the working class that animated the play in less prominent, though still important, roles.[20]

Belafonte and the young Sidney Poitier took classes and workshops at the actor's studio at the American Negro Theater. The playwright Alice Childress and the director Lloyd Richards worked there as well. The theater's most famous production, *Anna Lucasta*, was later produced on Broadway. The American Negro Theater was a financial cooperative where members shared both expenses and profits. Members who worked in productions outside of the ANT contributed 2 percent of their salaries to the cooperative.[21] At the ANT, Petry was in the center of black theater and surrounded by a number of politically minded young black artists. By decade's end many of her colleagues in the theater would be marked as Communists. Some were under investigation or had been asked to testify before the House Un-American Activities Committee.

In addition to making connections in the theater, Petry also acquired techniques that would help her to hone her craft as a writer. Petry later recalled, "Acting didn't really interest me—but what did interest me was to experience firsthand the way in which dialogue in a play furthers action."[22] She used every opportunity to enhance her craft. For instance, in the novella *In Darkness and Confusion,* she used dialogue and fast-paced narrative to change her readers' perceptions: what appears to be a mob becomes a crowd made up of individuals who express their frustration and anger at the conditions they face on a daily basis.

After the run of *On Strivers Row* ended, Petry once again had her nights and weekends free, but not for long. She took piano lessons and advanced courses in tailoring and taught an elementary course in writing business letters at the Harlem branch of the YWCA. She also took painting and drawing classes at the Harlem Community Art Center. At the center, located at 107 West 116th Street, Petry was no doubt exposed to the highly charged political energy of new fellow artists, and her desire to create complex portrayals of ordinary black people would likely have been nurtured and encouraged there. Her instructors might have included great black artists such as Aaron Douglas, Norman Lewis, and William H. Johnson, who all taught there. The Harlem Community Art Center opened on December 20, 1937, under the directorship of sculptor Augusta Savage. The painter Gwendolyn Bennett led the center from 1939 to 1944. Within a year of its opening, the center had enrolled more than 3,000 students.

Like the South Side Community Art Center in Chicago, the Harlem Community Art Center was one of the venues established by the Federal Art Project of the Works Progress Administration. Both centers played an important role in developing young black artists.[23] A young Jacob Lawrence took some of his first classes at the Harlem Community Art Center. Romare Bearden found his way there as well. Petry recalled that as an art student she concentrated on "people, landscapes . . . everything."[24] Petry's Connecticut landscapes and Harlem street scenes in her novels seemed to benefit greatly from her visual training at the art center. Her later novels are almost cinematic, and in the fifties she would go to Hollywood to a write a screenplay, *That Hill Girl*. Commissioned by Columbia Studios, the film was to have been a vehicle for Kim Novak, but it was never produced.

Black spaces were not the only ones that furthered and supported Petry's artistic efforts. She also attended Mabel Louise Robinson's workshop and course in creative writing at that other august Harlem institution, Columbia University. Petry recalled: "George was in the army; I was working for the *People's Voice* and trying to write short stories, and I was just getting back rejection slips." Following advice that she found in Arthur Train's autobiography, *My Day in Court*, she applied for and was accepted to Robinson's writing workshop. Robinson's Columbia workshops were legendary. She taught them for twenty-six years, and students who came through Robinson's class published over two hundred books. Petry later said: "There were only five people in that class, and they were all females; all the men had gone off to war. And so we literally did have her undivided attention. . . . She was truly interested in us, truly committed to our becoming writers."[25]

According to Petry, she learned many things from Robinson, the most important being how to incorporate "true" events into fiction. "They can't just be stuck in like raisins or plums or something. They have to be mixed in," Petry wrote.[26] This is a lesson she learned well; many of her stories and novels include incidents that she covered as a journalist or that were inspired by newspaper stories she read. Petry recalled that Robinson encouraged her students to read plays and go to the theater because plays told stories only in terms of dialogue. But most importantly, Petry credited Robinson's class with teaching her how to critique her own writing. The experience was to have a profound influence on her writing and her career. She dedicated her third and last novel, *The Narrows*, to Robinson.

While in Robinson's class, Petry finally began to publish her short stories. The network of black and left-wing magazines that published her first short stories helped to develop her reputation as a young writer before and immediately following the publication of *The Street* in 1946. The 1940s witnessed the birth of a number of very important little magazines that published the work of established and emerging black writers.

Among these were *Negro Quarterly*, for which Ralph Ellison served as managing editor; *Negro Story*; *Negro Digest*; and *Harlem Quarterly*.[27] Petry's fiction appeared in these magazines throughout the 1940s as well as in established publications like *The Crisis* and *Opportunity*. She also published in Popular Front publications such as *Common Ground*, *PM*, and *Cross Section*. These journals furthered the Popular Front's mission to produce a people's art.

Ann Petry was a prolific writer of short stories, and it was within that genre that she first sought to make her name. She began writing in the midst of an explosion of black short fiction. Black authors often chose to write short stories in the 1930s and the 1940s in an effort to target black audiences, since they believed that short stories appealed to black working-class readers with little time for reading full-length novels.[28] It was still the golden age of the short story in the mainstream press, with top magazines like the *Saturday Evening Post* paying top dollar for pieces by the luminaries of the day. In the black press, short stories were published in "little magazines." Like the more radical newspapers of the black press, little magazines helped to create a critical, even oppositional sensibility. A number of Petry's short stories appeared in these publications. And, like her contemporaries, Petry used the form to give voice to ordinary working people. A brief inventory of Petry's short fiction reveals three that were inspired by newspaper stories. Three are integrationist race-relation stories set in New England. Three are Harlem implosion stories where racial frustrations lead to violence turned inward, and one is a jazz story.[29]

When Houghton Mifflin discovered Petry and encouraged her to write a novel in 1943, she applied for the publishing house's literary fellowship. Houghton Mifflin granted her $2,400 in 1945. With this money and the $50 monthly stipend she received from her husband's allotment check, Petry quit her various jobs in order to devote her full attention to writing. George's absence gave her the time and space she needed to acquire training and to write, and his financial support helped to subsidize her efforts. She later recalled, "I began my first novel, writing every day from 9:00 a.m. to noon, and then stopping for an hour for lunch and writing from 1:00 p.m. to 2:30 or 3:00 P.M. every day." Some days an idea or an image would appear as she rode the subway. According to her daughter, "[Petry] said it might have been the jolting of the subway cars on the long ride but the information seemed to 'pop into my head.'"[30] Once she was home, a passage would unfurl from that simple image or idea. Petry's husband sometimes teased her that late-night subway trips always resulted in "some drunk" pouring out his life story to her.

Petry wrote the first chapter of *The Street* directly on the typewriter without revising anything. The rest of the book went through several drafts. As Petry later recalled: "I went over . . . the rest of it over and over and over again, simplifying it, testing the dialogue, the descriptions of people and places. I put all of my feelings, my sense of outrage into the book. I tried to include the sounds and the smells and sights of Harlem. I wanted a book that was like an explosion inside the head of the reader, a book that you couldn't put down once you'd started reading it. I tried to create a vivid sense of balance."[31] The result was a novel unlike any other in American literary history. From the very first page, Lutie Johnson, the novel's protagonist, is under assault by the natural and built environment, by white and black individuals, and by economic and political systems that have been historically built upon the exploitation and domination of people like Lutie.

Lutie is a Harlem resident who walks the same streets Petry walked, though she tends to spend more time below 125th than above. She is an ambitious single mother and domestic servant trying to move up in the ranks of civil servants. She believes in the American Dream and is certain that economic success and security await her if only she works hard enough. Lutie has chosen Benjamin Franklin as an intellectual ancestor and mentor, and as she walks the streets of Harlem, she contemplates the guidance Franklin offers in his *Autobiography*. Much of the novel documents her growing awareness that the ideas and ideals posited by Franklin and other Founding Fathers not only did not include her, but were based upon a foundation that depended upon her enslavement. It's no coincidence that one of the figures who helps to bring about Lutie's demise is named Junto, a name inspired by a mutual improvement society founded by Franklin in 1731. The Junto's membership was limited to white males, who not only helped to educate one another, but also helped each other gain financial independence. By engaging Franklin's *Autobiography*, Petry was asserting that Lutie's difficulties were not caused by a lack of work ethic, personal responsibility, or ambition; instead, it was white supremacy that had prevented women like Lutie from achieving the American Dream.

As Lutie—and Petry herself—realized, the fraught relationship between race, class, gender, and the founding principles of American democracy played out daily in the small, seemingly insignificant challenges of life in Harlem. For instance, Lutie is a consumer who is fully aware of the issues that Petry outlined in her call for Negro Women Incorporated—such as lack of access to adequate food and housing—but no such organization appears in the story. Petry put her own personal observations into Lutie's experience of Harlem. Lutie walks Eighth Avenue as Petry herself walked it, taking in the small stores along the way. Lutie notes, "All of them—the butcher shops, the notion stores, the vegetable stands—all of them sold the leavings, the sweepings, the impossible unsalable merchandise, the dregs and dross that were reserved especially for Harlem."[32] Harlem residents were forced to consume cheap goods, and as such they were also treated as if they were "the dregs and dross" of society. Finally, not only were they encouraged to buy this merchandise, but they were also encouraged to sell themselves cheaply as laborers and as sex objects.

Although Lutie first has the personal experience and then later the critical awareness of the larger overarching structures that limit her choices in consumer goods, housing, job opportunities for herself, and educational opportunities for her son, she does not have the opportunity to channel either that experience or that consciousness into organized political activity. She is too preoccupied with survival: an extra job, studying for a civil service exam, taking care of her child. Eventually she will think her talent for singing might be a way out. Singing is portrayed as an option for black women outside of prostitution

and domestic service, and yet containing remnants of both—
a form of serving white audiences by entertaining them and
putting one's sexuality on display.

Lutie's concern with survival keeps her from meetings like
those of the Harlem Riverside Defense Council or Negro
Women Incorporated, if she is even aware of their existence.
Petry allowed her character a limited experience of Harlem,
certainly one that was far narrower than her own. Lutie walks a
very circumscribed map of central Harlem confined by 116th
and 125th. She never visits Sugar Hill or Strivers Row. She
sees the cheap stores on Eighth Avenue, but she does not visit
the open-air market that Petry would later describe in an article about Harlem. She never encounters an activist preacher
like Adam Clayton Powell Jr., or people like Dollie Robinson,
Louise Thompson, Esther Cooper, and Ella Baker.

Petry refused to portray these failures as an indictment of
Lutie and her nonfiction sisters, but instead pointed out a basic
reality: the most committed organizations and individuals
were not always available to the people who needed them
most. And the forces that both confronted were ultimately far
more powerful than the efforts of individuals or organizations. Petry's commitment to realism insisted upon a portrayal
of Harlem life as it was experienced by most of its residents,
not just well-known artists and members of the black elite. She
was the sensitive activist, the ever-aware artist who was concerned with the people who may not have been touched by her
activism or her art. Petry realized that for characters like Lutie,
there was no way out. Lutie's circumstances demanded a fundamental change in the economic and political structure.

Petry portrayed Lutie's failures as the result of all the formations set up against her, those put into place without consideration for her well-being by people who could imagine her as nothing more than chattel. The contemporary society she inhabits is one that has inherited the very worst of the principles advanced by the Founding Fathers. Though formal slavery is over, Lutie is still viewed as a commodity for sale. She is the fictional sister of the large number of black women who, between 1940 and 1944, left domestic service and took advantage of the opportunity to pursue work as low-level civil servants or war industry workers. The number of black women employed as domestic servants decreased from 60 percent to 44 percent during this period as more varied jobs opened up for women in the war industry. Nonetheless, those who found work within the war industry were most often given custodial positions that mirrored domestic labor.[33]

Although *The Street* is primarily concerned with a single mother, black men are never far away. Petry, ever cognizant of George's experience in the military, gave voice to black men's frustration, especially during wartime. Boots Smith, Petry's fictional character, is not George Petry. A bandleader and Lutie's potential love interest, he lives outside the mainstream, refusing to participate in a straight and narrow life. Boots has worked as a Pullman Car porter, a highly coveted and politicized profession for black men, but chooses the life of a musician because of its relative freedom compared to other options available to black men. Like real-life figures such as Malcolm X and Dizzy Gillespie, Boots does not join the military. When asked if he wants to go to war, Boots responds, "Why should I?" He goes on to explain, "They hate Germans, but they hate me worse. If that wasn't so they wouldn't have a separate army for black men. . . . Sending a black army to Europe to fight Germans. Mostly with brooms and shovels." George Petry's experiences confirmed this view of what it meant to be a black soldier. He later asserted that German POWs were treated better than black soldiers. Nazi prisoners of war who were held on US military bases were allowed to dine with white soldiers in racially segregated mess halls. When Lena Horne performed at a southern camp, the audience was segregated and black soldiers were seated behind German POWs. Horne stepped off-stage, walked down the aisle past the whites, and sang directly to the black men in her audience.

Boots gives voice to Petry's disdain for the segregated military. While her new husband enlisted, served in a Jim Crow military, and suffered the daily humiliations that most black servicemen faced, Petry imagined a character, an outlaw figure, who dared to avoid the draft. But Petry acknowledged, even in her fiction, the diverse range of political thought among black Americans. Lutie uncritically believes in the American Dream and all of the national myths that accompany it. Boots, meanwhile, possesses a level of cynicism that makes it impossible for him to believe that the country is worth fighting for.[34]

While many young black men in real life may have felt the same way Boots, Gillespie, and Malcolm X did about the US military, most, like George, went on to serve in the military and displayed great loyalty while doing so. David Dinkins, mayor of New York City from 1990 to 1993; heavyweight boxing champion Joe Louis; and writer Albert Murray are but a few of the well-known African Americans who served with distinction. But there were just as many unknown and unnamed who would never fully get over the trauma of attending boot camp under the direction of racist officers or the treatment they received at home and abroad at the hands of bigots. These types of young men would appear in Petry's fiction—and the difficulties they faced would preoccupy most of black America throughout the war years. National civil rights organizations like the NAACP and the National Urban League joined the black press in an organized campaign against racial segregation in the military.

The Street eventually sold more than 1.5 million copies, becoming the first book by a black woman to surpass 1 million books sold and launching Petry as a literary celebrity. The novel was widely reviewed, and a number of articles and interviews with Petry appeared in the black and mainstream press. Given the success of novels such as Richard Wright's *Native Son,* Houghton Mifflin was optimistic, putting its full weight behind the novel. The publisher, expecting the book to attract a primarily black audience, created an extensive publicity campaign targeting black periodicals such as *Negro Digest, Ebony, Opportunity,* and *Phylon.* Petry's picture appeared on the cover of *Opportunity,* and *Ebony* published a glossy photo layout. Copies of the book were sent to a number of national organizations, including the National Council of Negro Women, the Brotherhood of Railroad Trainmen, the Council Against Intolerance in America, and the NAACP. The Urban League promised to issue pamphlets on Petry, and three of Harlem's bookstores held signing parties, including the National Memorial Bookstore, the Frederick Douglass Bookstore, and the Frances Reckling Book and Music Store. The same year, one of Petry's short stories, "Like a Winding Sheet," was selected for *The Best American Short Stories*, and the collection was dedicated to her. The New York Women's City Club honored her for her "exceptional contributions to the life of New York City."[35]

Following the publication of *The Street*, Petry became identified with a group of African American artists who were drawn to social realism, an aesthetic that expressed a leftist political philosophy and focused on working-class people and their concerns. Although social realism has been viewed as a phenomenon of the Depression era, African American artists and writers continued to work within this aesthetic well into the early years of the Cold War. These artists believed it was their responsibility to raise the democratic consciousness of their readers.[36] Among Petry's social realist contemporaries were visual artists John Biggers, Charles White, Hale Woodruff, Elizabeth Catlett, and Ernest Crichlow; poets Gwendolyn Brooks, Sterling Brown, Langston Hughes, Melvin Tolson, and Margaret Walker; and novelists William Attaway, Lloyd Brown, Willard Motley, and Richard Wright. The novelists saw fiction as the form that could best serve to educate and reform society.

In this way they inherited a great deal from earlier artists such as Zola, Dickens, and Dreiser, who were all among Petry's most cherished authors. Richard Rorty includes American writers like Dreiser, Sinclair Lewis, and John Steinbeck as part of the literary legacy of the American Left: they were writers who depicted social problems as a means of encouraging readers to address and alleviate them. If Lutie claimed Benjamin Franklin, Petry could claim all of these writers as her own literary ancestors.

Black social realists did not profess that the working classes were class-conscious or revolutionary, although, during the course of their novels and stories, their protagonists do seem to acquire a degree of critical consciousness. They portray them as a population with the potential, if they were enlightened and organized, to become revolutionary. Petry differed from her contemporaries in a few important ways, most notably in her willingness to provide a number of viewpoints in order to counter any sense of a monolithic black community, even among the working poor. Furthermore, her attention to gender, especially to the specific nature of black women's oppression, brought a new perspective to those marginalized black women who had been ignored or stereotyped in earlier black fiction and in the work of her male contemporaries.

During her years in Harlem, Petry began to develop her own aesthetic—an aesthetic she would elaborate upon more fully in an essay entitled "The Novel as Social Criticism" that appeared in *The Writer's Book* in 1950. In this essay, her most sustained critical statement, Petry defended the "sociological novel," which had come under great scrutiny during the years following World War II, especially because of its overt leftist politics. Just one year before her essay was published, a young James Baldwin had published his scathing critique of Harriet

Beecher Stowe's *Uncle Tom's Cabin* as well as *Native Son* by Wright—who was his mentor. According to Baldwin, the focus on protest in these novels took away from the creation of emotionally and psychologically complex black characters.

Petry addressed critiques like Baldwin's head-on in "The Novel as Social Criticism." She wrote, "Being a product of the twentieth century (Hitler, atomic energy, Hiroshima, Buchenwald, Mussolini, USSR) I find it difficult to subscribe to the idea that art exists for art's sake. It seems to me that all truly great art is propaganda, whether it be the Sistine Chapel, or La Gioconda, Madame Bovary, or War and Peace."[37] Petry argued for the continuing significance of sociological fiction, identified its deep roots in Western culture, and distanced it from charges of Marxist propaganda, but without denying the significance of Marxism. "Not all of the concern about the shortcomings of society originated with Marx," she wrote. "Though part of the cultural heritage of all of us derives from Marx, whether we subscribe to the Marxist theory or not, a larger portion of it stems from the Bible."[38] Petry situates Marx in the context of Western thought, saying his thought had influenced Western society in much the way Freud's had—one need not have read either to have experienced their influence. The same might be said of the Bible—although most westerners were even more familiar with the stories of the Bible than they were with the ideas of Freud or Marx, especially the Bible stories meant to inform our behavior and morality. And certainly, especially during the Cold War, even the most right wing of readers would not argue with the importance of biblical injunctions.

From here, Petry argues for the importance of sociological fiction in a number of ways. First, she grounds the tradition in the Bible, particularly the Old Testament story of Cain and Abel, whereby Cain asks God, "Am I my brother's keeper?" Petry also argues against art for art's sake while insisting upon the importance of craft, especially in the development of full, complex characters. According to Petry, that which distinguishes successful novels from their more didactic cousins is craftsmanship and the author's development of characterization and theme: "Once the novelist begins to manipulate his characters to serve the interests of his theme they lose whatever vitality they had when their creator first thought about them." "The Novel as Social Criticism," like Zora Neale Hurston's essays of the thirties, was an important early presentation of aesthetic theory by a black woman thinker. Along with Hurston, Petry helped to pave the way for novelist-critics like Toni Morrison.[39]

In spite of Petry's protests, the novel of social criticism did fall out of fashion with the emergence of writers such as Ralph Ellison and James Baldwin, whose first novels were published in 1952 and 1953, respectively. Baldwin and Ellison wrote formally complex, modernist works that focused on the individual psychology of their characters. Furthermore, in keeping with a rightward, more conservative, anti-Communist shift in American political life in general—and the mainstream civil rights movement in particular—neither writer launched major left-leaning critiques. Publishing companies and white liberal intellectuals found this work more to their liking, and the window of opportunity for the social realists quickly closed.

The Street is perhaps Petry's most complete literary example of what she argued for in "The Novel as Social Criticism," but the aesthetic principles she outlined there are apparent in all of her fiction. In one of her most highly crafted but least appreciated short stories, "In Darkness and Confusion," published in 1946, she tackled one of the most significant events to happen in New York during the war years—the Harlem Riot of 1943.

Suppose the day we spent walking through Harlem was Sunday, August 1, 1943. It was hot. That morning we read a story in the *Amsterdam News* about a black sergeant in Georgia who was executed because he'd gotten into an altercation with a state police officer. Say we have heard a number of stories about the mistreatment of black servicemen in the racist South. We may have attended services at one of the many Harlem churches—maybe the Reverend Adam Clayton Powell Jr.'s Abyssinian Baptist Church—but the pastor didn't preach because he was out of town. After church, we may have gone to see *Stormy Weather* with Lena Horne and Bill "Bojangles" Robinson at the RKO Alhambra at 126th and Seventh. Horne was becoming famous for the title song, which had previously been sung by Ethel Waters and Billie Holiday. Horne was the bronze pin-up for the brown boys overseas. In fact, they so loved her that the Marines of the 51st Defense Battalion named a gun after her in 1945. She was later considered for the role of Lutie in the film version of *The Street*, which was never made. Or, since this was Sunday, our day to relax, maybe we had planned to catch Cootie Williams and his band at the Apollo on 125th Street. Williams's band played both bebop and rhythm and blues,[40] and this made it an embodiment of the transitional nature of black urban life during the war years—a life still grounded in the advances and traditions of the first Great Migration and the New Negro movement but sitting on the verge of something new and consequential.

By seven, just before dusk, it is still very hot, and we start to hear a new rumor. It is about a soldier who has been shot and killed by a white cop at the Braddock Hotel on West 126th and Eighth Avenue. We knew the Braddock, because it is a favorite haunt of musicians, who sometimes rehearse downstairs. Carmen McRae and Sarah Vaughan are frequently there, and even stars like Dizzy Gillespie.

But tonight, mobs begin to form. Riots have already taken place in Los Angeles (the Zoot Suit Riots), Detroit (at the Sojourner Truth Houses), and Beaumont, Texas. We will later learn that the soldier, Private Robert Bandy, didn't die. He had been with his mother when he saw a white policeman, Officer James Collins, trying to arrest a young woman, Marjorie (Margie) Polite. The officer hit the young woman and Bandy intervened on her behalf. Collins shot Bandy in the shoulder. Bandy was taken to Harlem Hospital, where he was treated and released. But the rumor of a white cop shooting and killing a black soldier in uniform is unstoppable. It quickly spreads, igniting a powder keg of resentment over police brutality, maltreatment of black soldiers, residential discrimination, and a myriad other ills suffered by black Harlemites. Before the end of the day, it will take close to 7,000 New York City police officers and military police, along with as many members of the National Guard and a number of volunteers, to quell the riot. Mayor LaGuardia will ride the streets of Harlem throughout the night, speaking to the rioters through a bullhorn. He will close off the streets, order a curfew, and close bars and nightclubs. A number of black ministers will join him.

After two days of rioting, property damages were estimated at over $5 million, hundreds were arrested, and six people, all black, were dead. The streets were filled with debris from broken windows and looted stores. Communist leader Benjamin Davis proclaimed that Harlem's residents had "perfectly legitimate grievances" and sufficient reasons for the revolt, including the prevalence of police brutality on the streets of Harlem, even while the nation fought a war against fascism. Rev. Powell issued a statement blaming the riots on the "blind, smoldering and unorganized resentment against Jim Crow treatment of Negro men in the armed forces and the unusual high rents and cost of living forced upon Negroes in Harlem." A coalition of black leaders from politically moderate organizations, including the National Urban League, met with city officials in the days following the riots. While they agreed that the disturbances had turned into "outbreaks of hoodlumism," they nonetheless called attention to the social and economic conditions that led to the rioting.[41]

Ralph Ellison wrote about the riot in the *New York Post* in 1943, and then famously fictionalized it in *Invisible Man*, published in 1952. James Baldwin wrote about it in a 1955 work, *Notes of a Native Son*. And Langston Hughes penned a poem inspired by it, "The Ballad of Margie Polite," which appeared in the *Amsterdam News* just two months after the riot. It was a thirteen-stanza poem. Stanzas 1, 3, 5, and 7 were as follows:

> *If Margie Polite*
> *Had of been white*
> *She might not've cussed*
> *Out the cop that night.*
>
> . . .
>
> *A soldier took her part.*
> *He got shot in the back*
> *By a white cop—*
> *The soldier were black.*
>
> . . .
>
> *They taken Margie to jail*
> *And kept her there.*
> *DISORDERLY CONDUCT*
> *The charges swear.*
>
> . . .
>
> *She started the riots!*
> *Harlemites say*
> *August 1st is*
> *MARGIE'S DAY.*

About the riot, Petry later recalled, "I can remember walking through 125th Street when the street was filled with the shattered glass from the store windows. It made a crunching sound. I can still hear it."[42]

Petry used these vivid memories to inform her fictional account of the riots and the events that led up to them. William Jones, the protagonist of "In Darkness and Confusion," shares an apartment with his obese churchgoing wife, Pink, and her teenage niece, Annie May, a southern migrant who is discovering all the temptations of the city. Annie May was inspired by the young women Petry encountered in Harlem who were a bit younger than Lutie Johnson but, like her, also absent from the organizational meetings to which Petry devoted her time. However, young women like Annie May made their presence known on the streets of Harlem. Approaching three of them, Jones describes them with a tone of disdain:

> As far as he could see, they looked exactly alike. All three of them. And like Annie May. Too thin. Too much lipstick. Their dresses were too short and too tight. . . . He knew too, that [Annie May] didn't earn enough money to pay for all the cheap, bright-colored dresses she was forever buying. Her girl friends looked just like her and just like these girls. He'd seen her coming out of the movie houses on 125th Street with two or three of them. They were all chewing gum and they nudged each other and talked too loud and laughed too loud. They stared hard at every man who went past them.

Might these "too-too girls" be female counterparts of Ellison's zoot-suit-wearing jitterbugs that his protagonist encounters on the subway platform in *Invisible Man*? In an unsigned editorial just after the Harlem Riot of 1943, Ellison suggested that black leadership fails if it does not seek to solve the riddle of the zoot. He wrote, "Much in Negro life remains a mystery; perhaps the zoot-suit conceals profound political meaning; perhaps the symmetrical frenzy of the Lindy-hop conceals clues to great potential power." This is a riddle he himself seeks to unravel in *Invisible Man*, and one that would occupy brilliant thinkers after him.[43] The Lindy Hop and the emerging sound of bebop, according to Ellison, embodied the energies and frustrations of these young men—frustrations that led to the chaos and discontent of wartime race riots.

But let's linger a bit longer with the young women, the "too-too girls." We might ask, Who are they? What are their hopes, aspirations, dreams, and frustrations? What is their style? What songs do they sing as they work throughout the day to ease heartbreak or express a heart's longing? What music plays through their heads as they dress for a night out? What rhythms inspire their work? Imagine them: a flirtatious glance here, a familiar gesture there, hands on hips, head tilted. The spirit of black urban life was embodied by not only the zoot suiters, but also by the "too-too girls." With only a short passage in her story, Petry introduced them to the fictional page. She dared to represent them, and in so doing asked new questions about her time, place, and people.

For Jones—and in all likelihood, for Petry's readers—the young women are unfamiliar, unreachable, foreign, and just wrong. The refrain "too" suggests he resents their insistence, their exploding beyond the boundaries, their stepping outside the lines, their taking more from life than it tells them they dare have. They are boldly sexual, which he finds distasteful. He despises their dismissal of proper behavior and respectability. He contrasts them with his upstanding only son, Sam, a scholar athlete who first works as a redcap before joining the military. (Redcap was the nickname given to railroad porters who wore the red hats as part of their uniforms. Most railroad porters were black men. They were also members of the Union of Sleeping Car Porters founded by A. Philip Randolph. These were prestigious, sought-after jobs. Redcaps were greatly admired and respected in black communities throughout the United States.) Sam, the story's Negro soldier figure, is stationed down south in Georgia.

In Petry's story, Jones's son becomes a stand-in for Private Robert Bandy. After learning that his son has been court-martialed for shooting a racist officer, Jones, fed up with the streets he walks, his job, and Annie May, goes to a Harlem bar in an unnamed hotel on a hot August night in 1943. Petry doesn't name it, but this fictional hotel is based on the Braddock. Once there, Jones looks out into the lobby of the hotel and sees a black soldier in uniform, who reminds him of Sam, confronting a white police officer. He witnesses the event that provokes the Harlem Riot. Shortly thereafter, he finds himself in the crowd.

Here Petry's story becomes the story of the crowd, and Jones merely our touchstone to the larger entity. As the crowd continues to move, Jones turns to spot a young thin girl and realizes it's Annie May holding a nude mannequin by the waist and hurtling it through the air. Looking at Annie May, "He felt now that for the first time he understood her. She had never had anything but badly paying jobs working for young white women who probably despised her. She was like Sam on that bus in Georgia. She didn't want just the nigger end of things." In darkness and confusion, Jones identifies with Annie May and he abolishes the distinction he had been making between them—between the "good" Sam and the "bad" Annie May. Similar fates awaited both of them; neither of them had any future. Both of them are only guilty of trying to assert their dignity, of standing defiantly in the face of old racist practices that confront them on a daily basis. Petry makes the ordinary, anonymous participants of the Harlem riots the central figures of literary fiction. This is her major contribution as an artist: to give voice and complexity to those people who remain nameless in official accounts. She portrays their humanity, their frustrations, their anger and fear. She gives them names. Many people wrote about the riots. Few wrote about the rioters with such compassion and detail.

Young men and women like Sam and Annie May represented a new generation of African Americans. They were unwilling to tolerate second-class citizenship, unwilling to wait for the slow process of incremental change. Annie May is a fictional representative of the women described by a *New York Times* article that appeared on August 3, 1943, entitled "500 Are Arraigned in Harlem Looting: 100 Women Among Prisoners Crowding Courts After Night Disorders." The story's first line reads: "More than 500 prisoners, among them 100 women, many of them carrying the loot they had at the time of

Police arrest young women during the riots in Harlem, 1943. Copyright Brown Brothers, Sterling, Pennsylvania.

their arrest, were arraigned during the day and evening yesterday. . . . Many of the defendants were youths. Several wore zoot suits." Records from the Harlem Magistrate's Office do show that more young women, like Hughes's Margie Polite, were arrested for "disorderly conduct" on the night of the riot than on any other night preceding or following it—however, I have not been able to locate a record of the 100 women reported arrested by the *Times*. Perhaps they were arraigned in different magistrates' offices, but they seem to have quietly disappeared into the Harlem night.[44]

Although Petry wrote "In Darkness and Confusion" just after the riot, she could not find a publisher for it until 1946. She initially submitted it to *The Crisis*, a journal that had previously published her fiction. However, the editor, James Ivy, rejected it because of the language, which he encouraged her to keep while she sought other venues for publication.[45]

Harlem would not immediately recover from the riot. A number of businesses never reopened. Harlem nightlife especially took a hit: fewer white New Yorkers were now willing to risk a trip to Harlem's famed nightclubs and ballrooms. Finally and most importantly, many members of the black middle class also began a quiet exodus to the outer boroughs.

Petry lived in Harlem for only a few years after the riots. Sometime after George's return from the army, the couple relocated to Bronx Park East. Many middle-class African Americans began to leave, relocating, like the Petrys, to the Bronx, or to Queens. Petry would continue to write, and she still set many of her stories in Harlem, but her next two novels would be set in New England.

Early critics considered Petry part of the Richard Wright school of naturalist black fiction—a designation she deeply resented. Wright was the towering black literary figure of the time, and the success of his work certainly created the audience and market that would read Petry's work. He never served as her mentor, and he never seems to have read her work for publishing houses, as he did Gwendolyn Brooks's poetry. Petry later noted that while she read and admired Wright, Baldwin, and especially Ellison, she had never met any of them. She was part of a group of writers whose reach went beyond that of Wright. Petry, like Chicago's Gwendolyn Brooks, found inspiration in the lives of ordinary working-class black people, especially migrants and women. To modernist, urban landscapes, these writers added black women as walkers of the city.[46]

Petry's introduction of figures like Lutie and the "too-too girls" helped to give voice to black women who remained invisible to much of American society. As such, her fictional characters might join the sound of the young Dinah Washington in giving us a more textured understanding of the time. The epitome of the too-too girl, singer Dinah Washington—Miss D—was a child of the Great Migration and the Great Depression. Deeply steeped in gospel, she was first dubbed a blues singer and then a rhythm and blues pioneer. She was both and more. She was a capable interpreter of the blues, country and western, pop tunes, and jazz standards. She joined the Lionel Hampton Orchestra and eventually made Harlem her home. Like Petry with her "too-too girls," Washington exploded beyond genre and category. Hers was a sexually confident, insistent, and bold voice. In her music and her style, Washington captured the energy, the spirit, and the setting that animate Petry's fiction.

Even though she left Harlem soon after the war ended, Petry's most prolific decade was clearly the result of her deep involvement in and engagement with the neighborhood. Her literary celebrity soared with the publication of *The Street*. When her essay "The Novel as Social Criticism" appeared in the *Writer's Book*, she was published alongside the likes of W. H. Auden, Pearl S. Buck, and Lionel Trilling. Translations of *The Street* appeared in a number of languages including Spanish. The interest of foreign readers is evidence of Petry's widespread literary significance during this time. Petry recalled, "I became famous, a celebrity, almost overnight." However, she grew to disdain the fame she'd acquired. "After the publication of *The Street*," she said, "I began to feel as though I were public property. I was beleaguered by all the hoopla, the interviews, the invitations to speak." She left New York, and, to a certain degree, the center of her literary life, when she and George returned to Old Saybrook in 1948. There they purchased an old sea captain's house, built in 1790. Petry gave birth to her only child, a beautiful baby girl named Elisabeth, the following year. Petry would live, write, and raise her daughter in Old Saybrook until her death in 1997.[47]

Petry never suggested that her departure from the limelight and from New York may have been influenced by the nation's changing political climate. There is no FBI file on Petry, and she doesn't seem to have been personally sought out by Hoover or by the House Un-American Activities Committee. The very fact that she was hired by Hollywood to write a screenplay for *That Hill Girl*, a feature-length vehicle for blonde bombshell Kim Novak, during the height of the Red Scare suggests that no one believed her to have been a Communist. However, many of her former colleagues, contemporaries, and friends were. Adam Clayton Powell Jr. broke all ties with his Communist allies in 1947. Benjamin Davis, the black Communist city councilman from Harlem for whom Petry expressed support as late as 1949, was sent to prison under the Smith Act, and Marvel Cooke, her friend and colleague at the *People's Voice*, was subpoenaed by Joseph McCarthy in 1953. Two of the men Petry most admired, W. E. B. Du Bois and Paul Robeson, both lost their passports and were harassed by the FBI.

Harlem had lost some of its glitter; like many other black urban communities, with the Housing Act of 1949 the Black Mecca fell victim to urban renewal, which included the development of high-rise housing projects and the destruction of a number of neighborhood institutions. A heroin epidemic ensued. Harlem lost much of its radical and intellectual leadership and much of its middle class. After the war, middle-class African Americans met with increased opportunity for mobility as other areas of the city opened up to black residents, and many of those who could move did so. Those who moved found opportunities for homeownership and entry into the middle class.[48]

The American Left and the black poor did not fare well during the Cold War. McCarthyism and the Red Scare changed African American politics in New York, as figures such as FBI director Hoover and Senator McCarthy targeted the radical wing of the Left. They challenged the coalition between the labor and civil rights movements, tempered the call of black leaders for economic justice, and sought to silence vocal street protests and grassroots organizing.[49] With the rise of McCarthyism, calls for economic justice often were deemed Communist propaganda. Urban renewal efforts to redevelop areas by "eliminating blight," "clearing slums," and building high-rise public housing projects also led to the disruption of the community's networks and the isolation and immobilization of many of its poorer members.

Petry's final piece of writing to come out of her Harlem years would be the gorgeously illustrated essay "Harlem" that appeared in *Holiday* magazine in 1949. Written after she'd left Harlem, the essay closes with a pessimistic vision of New York, a place upon which the sun seemed to have set:

> Harlem has been studied and analyzed by sociologists, anthropologists, and politicians. It has been turned and twisted, to the right and to the left, prettied up and called colorful and exotic, defamed and labeled criminal. Sometimes its past has been glorified, more often it has been censured. But looked at head on, its thousand faces merge into one—the face of a ghetto. In point of time it belongs back in the Middle Ages. Harlem is an anachronism—shameful and unjustifiable, set down in the heart of the biggest, richest city of the world.[50]

Here Petry contributes to a "Harlem as Ghetto" discourse that dominated mainstream representations of the neighborhood for decades. Alternatively, a new generation of activist artists like Lorraine Hansberry, Maya Angelou, Abbey Lincoln, Louise Merriwether, and Toni Cade Bambara followed in Petry's footsteps and found inspiration in the Black Mecca's social complexity, cultural vibrancy, and political energy.

CHAPTER THREE

ROLLIN' WITH MARY LOU WILLIAMS

By late autumn 1943, Harlem faced an uncertain future. It would never fully recover from the riot. Whites, who had been an important source of income, stopped patronizing its nightlife. Eventually, many of the residents of Sugar Hill moved to places like St. Albans, Queens, and the Bronx. Some of the buildings that had been damaged during the riots remained empty of occupants for years. The scourge of heroin and gang violence began to overwhelm Harlem's streets. Eventually, urban renewal efforts would transplant large numbers of Harlem's black poor from tenements to high-rise housing projects, thereby contributing further to the concentration of poverty.

Nonetheless, the sense of political optimism had not completely vanished, as was evident when, on October 24, 1943, the fourth Sunday of the month, close to 4,000 "too-too girls" and their companions found their way to the Golden Gate Ballroom at 140th and Lenox. New York would hold its first Fashion Week that fall, a gathering of designers, fashion editors, and buyers—fashion industry insiders all. Uptown, the "too-too girls" set their own trends, and the streets of Harlem were their runways. That night, some of them wore softly tailored suits with nipped waists and round collars; others donned shirtwaist dresses with thin fabric belts. Pompadours and platform pumps seemed to send them soaring. The sidewalk outside the Golden Gate filled with young couples and groups of young men and women, all anticipating the evening. The occasion: a political rally in support of African American Communist Benjamin J. Davis Jr., a candidate for city council.[1]

On October 16, 1943, a full-page ad had run in the *Amsterdam News*:

THRILLING—SENSATIONAL
—INSPIRING—COLOSSAL

. . .

TERRIFIC ENTERTAINMENT
TEDDY WILSON
PRESENTS

ALL STAR VICTORY SHOW

IN TRIBUTE TO

BENJ. J. DAVIS, JR.
CITY COUNCIL CANDIDATE.

The ad featured photographs of Fredi Washington, Coleman Hawkins, Paul Robeson, Billie Holiday, and Mary Lou Williams. Tickets ranged from 55 cents to $2.50. That same issue ran an article about the planned event.

After graduating from Harvard Law School in 1929, Benjamin Davis had opened a legal office in Atlanta, where he had represented Angelo Herndon, who faced the death penalty for simply leading a protest demonstration. Stunned by the bitter racism he confronted in court, Davis joined the Communist Party. It was the party's support for and defense of Herndon— as well as the Scottsboro Boys, nine young black men indicted for the rape of two white women—that helped to garner the party such widespread respect in many black communities during the thirties and forties. Consequently, Davis was already an admired figure when he relocated to Harlem in 1935. In New York he edited the journal *Negro Liberator* and worked on the staff of the *Daily Worker*. By 1937, he had become a secretary of the Harlem Division of the Communist Party. Within a few years, Davis was one of the most popular political figures in Harlem. He was a leader who gave voice to the community's concerns and placed their plight in the context of larger national and global struggles. Davis saw "perfectly legitimate grievances" as the cause of the riots of 1943, including an increase in police brutality against blacks even as black soldiers fought against the fascists abroad.

By the time he ran for Powell's council seat, Davis had received the endorsement of the clergyman congressman and a bevy of Harlem's religious, civic, and political leaders. Cultural figures, including the writers Richard Wright and Langston Hughes, and actress Fredi Washington had also endorsed him. Poet Countee Cullen joined Ben Gold, president of the Fur Worker's Union, and Ferdinand Smith, secretary of the National Maritime Union, as a vice chairman of the nonpartisan committee to elect Ben Davis to the City Council of New York. Audley Moore, who would later be known as Queen Mother Moore, served as campaign manager. Moore is best known for her black nationalist politics, but at the time she was a leading black leftist. In the 1940s, ideological lines were not as harshly drawn between leftists and black nationalists; they were united in their commitment to the black freedom struggle. The brilliant pianist Teddy Wilson—the "Marxist Mozart"—chaired the Artists Committee. As pianist at Café Society and a widely respected musician, Wilson had helped to further Billie Holiday's career by featuring her as vocalist on a number of his recordings. He was able to successfully organize his fellow artists to appear at the rally in support of Davis's candidacy.

Two hours before the show started, the fire department had to close the doors because the ballroom was already filled to capacity. According to Davis, another 5,000 people stood outside the ballroom awaiting entrance. The committee quickly rented another hall six blocks away, the Renaissance, at 121 West 138th Street, and over 2,000 people came to hear the entertainers give a second show.

Musicians Coleman Hawkins, Hazel Scott, Count Basie, Lucky Roberts, Art Tatum, Jimmie Lunceford, and Mary Lou Williams; vocalists Billy Daniels, Billie Holiday, Lena Horne,

Josh White, and Ella Fitzgerald; and dancers Helen Tamiris and Pearl Primus were among the featured performers. There was even a performance by the Swa-Hili Dance Group "in Native African Dances." Fredi Washington served as mistress of ceremonies. Adam Clayton Powell Jr. roused the crowd with his opening remarks: "The will of the anti-Fascists, anti-Christian Frontiers and anti–Ku Klux Klan will send Benjamin J. Davis, Jr., to the City Council on November 2." Paul Robeson introduced Davis, remembering their long friendship, which had started when Robeson's Rutgers football team played against Davis's Amherst College team. (Davis had been the star of the team and was named "All Eastern Tackle" his senior year.) Hazel Scott received a roar of applause, not only because of her performance but also because of her $100 contribution to Davis's campaign ($1,333 in today's dollars). The cast of the Broadway play *Oklahoma* pledged $100 each to the campaign. And labor leader Elizabeth Gurley Flynn joined others of note on the platform. The *People's Voice* reported that the event "brought out more top flight stars than have ever honored any political candidate in the history of Harlem." According to the *Amsterdam News*, the artists "gave from the heart in a thrilling performance for a cause close to their hearts."[2]

In November 1943, Harlem sent Benjamin Davis, a Communist leader, to the New York City Council to represent their interests. On November 11, 1943, shortly after the election, a *New York Times* headline read "Democrats Margin in New Council Cut, 'Left' Forces Gain." Fellow Communist Peter V. Cacchione of Brooklyn joined Davis on the council. Davis noted that it was "crystal clear" that he had not been elected by Harlem alone or by the Communist Party alone. Davis had been elected by a coalition of voters who crossed religious, ethnic, and racial boundaries.[3]

When Davis returned to the Golden Gate Ballroom to deliver his first report on the city council, Count Basie, Teddy Wilson, Billie Holiday, Pearl Primus, Josh White, and Mary Lou Williams provided the entertainment again. In 1945, Davis won reelection with the second-highest vote ever received by a councilman. However, in 1949, he was expelled from the council. Tried and convicted, along with other Communists, under the Smith Act for conspiring to overthrow the US government, he was imprisoned, and he was not released until 1954. But Harlemites and their beloved celebrities refused to give up on Davis and continued to hold rallies in support of him even after his arrest. As late as 1949, Ann Petry wrote that Harlemites had "voted for Ben Davis because [they] felt he would never sell Harlem down the river," not because they were members of the Communist Party.[4] For Petry, Davis's commitment to black people, particularly those who were economically disadvantaged, endeared him to Harlem. They believed he would fight for their concerns and that he would not comply with policies that were not in their best interest. For them, his racial loyalties were more significant than his party affiliation.

The artists who performed at the events in support of Davis's candidacy more than likely shared these sentiments. They were not just the black community's most popular stars; with the exception of Count Basie and Ella Fitzgerald, most of the musicians were also affiliated with Café Society, which meant that they were likely staunch supporters of progressive causes. Teddy Wilson drew on his colleagues at Café Society, and the club's owner, Barney Josephson, encouraged his artists to be involved in political and civic events.

Mary Lou Williams was one such artist. Williams performed at Café Society nightly, and the club quickly became the nexus of her political, social, and creative life. Mary Lou and other performers from Café Society performed at a number of benefits. According to Williams, "Josh White had just joined the show . . . and we used to do sometimes 2 or 3 benefits per night."[5] These might be performances for soldiers at the Canteen on 44th Street or benefits for war relief, war orphans, political rallies, or other causes.

The Davis rally was the beginning of Mary Lou Williams's political activity.[6]

Of her political involvement, Williams later said, "There's not one musician I think would be in any kind of political anything if they weren't disturbed about the race, as being abused and whatnot, [and] trying to help the poor."[7] A child of the black poor, Williams believed they suffered from the twin evils of racism and poverty and that they were in need of special assistance. Williams remained deeply concerned about and committed to the plight of black Americans, especially the black poor, for the rest of her life. There were rumors she hosted Communist Party cell meetings in her Harlem apartment. It is unclear whether these rumors were true. But, although she sympathized with the Communist cause, and may have generously opened up her home to artists and activists who needed a place to meet, she was never a member of the Communist Party.

Most importantly, more so than Primus or Petry, Williams's passion for racial and economic justice was as spiritually driven as it was politically motivated. In fact, one cannot separate her spiritual quest from her political and philanthropic activities. By the early 1940s, she had not yet found a religion or a denomination to which to direct her spiritual yearnings. Nonetheless, her sense of spirituality, deeply informed by a kind of organic mysticism, called her to act in the world to alleviate human suffering. Unlike Petry and Primus, Williams did not always do so through organized efforts; in fact, most often she was engaged in individual, one-on-one efforts to free people of debt, addiction, violence, and homelessness.

By the time she moved to Sugar Hill in Harlem during the summer of 1943, Williams was already an established star in the black community. Black newspapers across the country documented her move to the city as well as her residency at Café Society. (It should be remembered that papers such as the *Pittsburgh Courier*, the *Chicago Defender*, and the *Baltimore Afro-American* had national distribution, so the news they reported was the news of black America.) When Williams moved to Harlem, the *Amsterdam News* reminded readers that "she is an Immortal of Jazz, one of the best female pianists in the business, and one of the top arrangers and composers regardless of sex."

Publicity photo, 1946. Courtesy of the Mary Lou Williams Collection, Institute for Jazz Studies, Rutgers University.

A child prodigy, Williams had proven herself to be a gifted musician, composer, and arranger long before settling in New York. Born Mary Elfrieda Scruggs, the second of eight children, on May 8, 1910, in Atlanta, Georgia, she was recognized early for her musical and spiritual gifts. Williams emerged from the womb with a veil, a thin membrane of placenta, thought by African Americans to be a sign of the child's clairvoyance. "I used to hear so many stories about spooks and ghosts," she remembered. "Seemed like I picked up on that when I was about two or three years old because my mother was afraid to take me out anywhere with us."[8] Early on the young girl experienced visions. Blessed from birth with a psychic sensibility, Williams would always link her musical gift to her deep spirituality.

At age three, Williams stunned her mother, herself a talented musician (though not a professional one), when she played melodies on the piano that she'd heard. Mary Lou, on her mother's lap at the piano, played the notes she had just watched her mother play, and it shocked her mother so much that she dropped her.[9] An introspective child, Williams possessed a complex inner life that helped her to see both the significance of her musical gift and the role it might play in helping her make her way to a better life than that into which she was born. Williams always possessed a sense of self far beyond what might have been expected for a young person in her situation. At best, a young black woman born into poverty might have worked as a domestic servant for most of her life. A musically talented one might have become a highly respected church musician. Had she acquired education, she might have become a teacher. As an entertainer, she might have acquired a modicum of success and fame. But Williams's ambitions went beyond all of this. She was confidently aware of her genius, and throughout her life she sought opportunities to express it fully.

Williams described her family's home in Atlanta as "a wooden frame house near swampy woods" where her mother and grandmother went on "regular weekend drinking sprees."[10] In fact, Williams's mother spent the week as a live-in domestic servant. If she enjoyed partying on Saturday night, she also regularly attended church on Sunday morning. There she served as pianist and organist. Eventually, both Williams's mother, Virginia Burley (who married Williams's stepfather, Fletcher Burley), and her grandmother, Anna Jane, earned money as laundresses.

Williams hid under the bed when her great-grandparents recounted stories about slavery, but she heard the tales nonetheless. From these stories she learned about the history of her people and their music, and for the rest of her life she saw black music as the deepest expression of black history. This association drove her sense of purpose and mission as well as her pedagogy. In a number of essays, both published and unpublished, Williams insisted that "jazz began with the spirituals." She wrote, "The black American Slaves were taken to church. They learned the hymns of the white people. Soon they began to create their own psalms or hymns. These became known as the spirituals. This is the first music that was later to develop into what we know as jazz."[11] Years later, she would have her friend David Stone Martin create an illustration of a black music tree with its roots in slavery and suffering.

Williams had no knowledge of her father, Joseph Scruggs, until years later. As she explained, "I was born out of wedlock, a common thing not only for black people, but also whites in the South." Eventually, she took the name of her stepfather, and throughout her life she thought of Fletcher Burley as her daddy. Burley nurtured Williams's musical gift, taught her the blues, and bought her her first player piano. On the player piano she heard and learned from the masters, people like Jelly Roll Morton and James P. Johnson. Before long she became a student of the Atlanta native Jack Howard. Later she said of him, "I like Jack Howard because he played such a strong piano he could break up all the pianos and as a baby I started playing like that. I think I got the masculine quality [of playing] from him." But for the most part, Williams was a self-taught pianist who learned by listening and playing. She learned to play in a variety of music styles from the player piano, including Harlem stride, boogie-woogie, waltzes, and light opera. She was also aware of the black religious music that permeated her surroundings.[12]

Unlike Petry and Primus, who grew up far removed from the racism and violence of the South, Williams experienced this prejudice firsthand. Williams certainly did not grow up in a family of middle-class professionals like Petry. She did escape the South. When she was five years old, she and her family joined the first wave of black migration, moving to Pittsburgh in 1915. Nevertheless, some of Williams's earliest memories were of racial violence. She retained images of lynching and of seeing a man's head "split open with an ax."[13] In Pittsburgh, white neighbors threw bricks into their windows and harassed her family, who lived with the constant threat of physical abuse. If that were not enough, lighter-skinned blacks were prejudiced against the chocolate brown child as well. Williams's great-grandfather was nearly white, with blond hair, and her great-grandmother, Matilda, was believed to be part Native American. According to Williams, Matilda, the most powerful figure in the family (especially after the death of her husband), was a color-struck woman who beat her dark-skinned grand-children more often than she did the lighter ones.

From the moment Williams discovered the piano, she could not be dragged away from it. The music became her refuge from poverty and maternal indifference. In Williams's memory, her mother was a cool, distant figure who never came to hear her play after she became famous. Her older sister Mamie, four years her senior, acted as her caregiver and confidante. Williams's younger siblings and her niece Bobbie Ferguson dispute this characterization of Virginia Burley.[14] In the begin-ning of Williams's life, Virginia was a single mother who had to work two jobs to care for her children. Once in Pittsburgh, though married, Burley continued to work long hours, and she had a number of other children.

In Pittsburgh, Williams earned the nickname "the little pi-ano girl of East Liberty." She played around town at parties for the city's elite, for funerals, and at silent films. She was even discovered by neighborhood prostitutes, who paid her to play in the local brothel. So, like Billie Holiday, who started out as an errand girl doing housework, eventually singing for money in Baltimore brothels, Williams found that her talent brought her paying brothel gigs. Unlike Holiday, however, Williams never became one of the working girls. In fact, her stint in the brothel didn't last long: instructed to peep through a view hole and play for the entire sexual encounter, she quit when one such encounter went on too long.

When she wasn't playing the piano at home or on her many local gigs, Williams attended Lincoln School, where she excelled in music and mathematics. From Lincoln she went to Westinghouse High School. Westinghouse boasted an array of important former students, pianists all: Ahmad Jamal, Billy Strayhorn, and Erroll Garner among them. Williams attended for only one term. During the summer of her twelfth year, in 1922, Williams joined the tent show "Buzzin' Harris and His Hits and Bits," and thus began her time on the black vaudeville circuit. During summer break, Williams's mother agreed to let her go on tour. By that time, she'd already earned a professional reputation in her hometown; been squired around the city's nightlife by an uncle figure, Roland Mayfield; and begun to develop into the beautiful young woman she would become. "At the age of 12 I looked like 18," she later said. Protected by Mayfield and her stepfather, she escaped numerous attempts by men to seduce and even rape her. When the opportunity to join Buzzin' Harris's outfit came along, she gladly jumped at it.

In spite of her multiple musical gifts, Williams had not learned to read music, a skill she wouldn't develop until a few years later, when she wanted to write down the sounds she heard in her head. Andy Kirk, tuba player and bandleader of the Twelve Clouds of Joy, and Johnny Williams, the show's saxophonist bandleader, helped her to transcribe them. Johnny Williams became her mentor and, eventually, her husband.

Bitten by the show-business bug, Williams eventually joined Andy Kirk's Twelve Clouds of Joy, an important territory band that toured the Southwest. Territory bands traveled within a designated area, transporting new musical styles along the way. Along with Benny Moten's Kansas City Orchestra, Andy Kirk's Twelve Clouds of Joy helped to nationalize the Kansas City sound, a highly rhythmic blues-based style of jazz that first developed in Kansas City, Missouri. Williams traveled extensively with the Kirk band and gained a reputation as an important and gifted musician. In her capacity as soloist and arranger, she soon became known as "The Lady Who Swings the Band." She'd reached her peak with the Kirk band when she began to set her sights on New York. She also divorced her first husband, and on December 10, 1942, she married the trumpeter Harold "Shorty" Baker. Williams and Baker began an affair when both were working for Kirk, and while Mary Lou was still married to John Williams. By this time, John and Mary Lou were married in name only.

Baker left the Kirk band first, to play with Duke Ellington, and Williams eventually followed him. During this time, Williams wrote arrangements for Duke Ellington and Benny Goodman. She wrote the rollicking "Roll 'Em," a blues-based boogie-woogie tune, for the Goodman orchestra. The tune moves through space and time with a momentum and sense of joy that surely sent dancers soaring. She also arranged a number of tunes for Ellington, including "Trumpet No End" and "Blue Skies."

Throughout much of their brief time together, Baker was on the road with Ellington. In late 1943 or early 1944, Baker was drafted into the military.[15] Williams, desperate for a little stability, found an apartment for them in Harlem, #21 at 63 Hamilton Terrace. But Baker would never live there. Williams, excited about the possibility of a stable gig and eager to create a home for herself and her husband, moved in, but the marriage did not survive the war. Although Williams and Baker never legally divorced, Baker did not share Williams's life after the move. Nonetheless, the move to New York did bring the much-needed stability to Williams's life that she had sought. She had been on the road since she was twelve or thirteen years old. Williams lived at Hamilton Terrace throughout her time in New York and maintained the apartment after she left for Europe in 1952. She would continue to live there throughout the rest of her life, keeping it even after moving to Durham, North Carolina, in the 1980s, when she began to teach at Duke University.

Hamilton Terrace is located near 144th and St. Nicholas Avenue, in a neighborhood known as Sugar Hill. Bound by 155th Street to the north, 145th to the south, Edgecombe Avenue to the east, and Amsterdam Avenue to the west, Sugar Hill was home to many of Harlem's most prosperous and prominent citizens, including W. E. B. Du Bois and Duke Ellington. Describing Sugar Hill in the 1940s, Ann Petry wrote, "There is a moneyed class, which lives largely in and around the section known as the Hill. . . . The Hill suggests that Harlem is simply a pleasant and rather luxurious part of Manhattan."[16] In an essay on Sugar Hill in the *New Republic*, Langston Hughes explicitly stated what Petry implied. His wasn't a celebration of black achievement, but an effort to point out the contradictory experiences of Sugar Hill residents, always a minority, and that of other, poorer Harlemites.

Elegant and secured with a doorman, Williams's building housed her small, sunlit, one-bedroom apartment. She painted the kitchen lemon yellow and furnished the bedroom with two twin-sized Hollywood beds, upholstered in pink. She wrote music and kept up with correspondence in the bedroom. The apartment also had cabinets and files that held her compositions and arrangements as well as important papers and the essays and other writings she published. The heart of the apartment was the small living room, where a small upright Baldwin piano stood. On top of the piano she had placed various knickknacks, vases, and photos. Photographs taken by William P. Gottlieb in 1947 show Williams entertaining musician friends in this apartment. Dizzy Gillespie, Tadd Dameron, Jack Teagarden, and others surround Williams or Hank Jones as they play. Sometimes they are all seated in front of the piano engaged in conversation; at other times, they play cards on a small table that sits near the instrument. Williams had purchased a white rug for the center of the room, and she and her friends often sat there on the floor, listening to records on a portable record player.

Jack Teagarden, Dixie Bailey, Mary Lou Williams, Tadd Dameron, Hank
Jones, Dizzy Gillespie, and Milt Orent in Mary Lou Williams's apartment,
New York, August 1947. Photo by William P. Gottlieb.

In short, Williams made a home at Hamilton Terrace. Her
marriage ended, but she created her own family and community. The apartment became a salon for musicians, writers,
painters, journalists, and photographers. The younger musicians, such as Dizzy Gillespie, Thelonious Monk, and Bud
Powell, who pioneered the bebop revolution, were especially
welcome. They would find the door open, an inviting pot on
the stove, and, when she was there, Williams—as mentor, collaborator, and friend. They respected and admired her as an
elder in the music world and a model artist.

Williams's status as a single, childless woman, as well as
the stability afforded by her move to New York, helped to stim-

ulate one of her most exciting and productive periods, ushering in a new phase of artistic creativity and political activity.
The crowds, the vibrancy, and the excitement of the city found
its way into her music. The city's institutions—its libraries,
museums, and performance venues—offered material and inspiration. The marriage of progressive political activism and
innovative art forms provided a space for her own creative
growth and political maturation to occur. In other words, the
city served as an incubator for the further development of her
inherent musical gifts, her spiritual sensibilities, and her desire for social justice. It is during this period that we see the beginnings of the spiritual, musical, and activist flowering that
would occur in later decades.

Interestingly, at a time in life when most women were creating a home space and nurturing husbands and children,
Mary Lou was creating a space that nurtured her own creativity and that of her fellow artists. As a result, she embarked upon
a phase of her life characterized by fecund creativity grounded
in place and community, as if she had been searching for a way
to give back and had discovered a way to better her community
and her nation. Her time in New York was not without its difficulties. Williams's later involvement with gamblers and other
denizens of the Harlem night revealed the underside of New
York's glamour, but Williams would use this to fuel her creativity and her humanitarian efforts.

During the 1940s, while writing and arranging music,
Williams also wrote prose essays about her music, mentored
and taught, recorded a number of albums, and performed

throughout the city. On many nights, she took the subway, composing music in her head as the train rattled through the tunnel headed to The Village. "I get my inspiration from modern things," Williams said, and she counted the subway as one of them. Just as the subway gave Petry images and ideas for her fiction, it delivered musical ideas and sounds to Williams. She would arrive at the club "with the complete arrangement worked out."[17]

Duke Ellington's "Take the A Train" is more famous, but Williams penned and recorded her own tribute to the famous subway line: "Eighth Avenue Express," which she recorded in 1944.[18] The choo-choo of the drummer and Williams's hard left hand drive this highly energetic boogie-woogie blues song. The piece is complete with train stops and announcements beckoning arrival in Harlem.

Williams opened at Café Society sometime in June 1943 to a full house. "My opening, the people were standing upstairs," she recalled. "Pearl Primus, my favorite dancer, was also in the show," she later wrote. "I don't know of any other place quite like it. I must say that Barney was the greatest nightclub owner in the business. He'd give most anybody that was talented a chance to make good by putting them in the club for a long run. If they didn't become great then they just weren't good to begin with."[19] Williams, of course, would become great. Years later, in the seventies, Josephson jump-started Williams's career again when he booked her at The Cookery, a club he opened in the 1970s.

Williams befriended many of the other artists at Café Society, including Primus and Imogene Coca, but her most enduring friendship was with fellow pianist Hazel Scott. Some thought that there was a professional rivalry between the two, but this was far from true. *Time* magazine even tried to stoke such a rivalry by comparing the two women—without naming Scott, who was known for her glamour, her sexy presentation, her low-cut gowns, and her "swinging the classics" style. The July 26, 1943, issue of *Time* noted that Mary was "no kitten on the keys." The reporter went further, writing, "She was not selling a pretty face or a low décolletage, or tricky swinging of Bach or Chopin. She was playing the blues, stomps, and boogie-woogie in the native Afro-American way—an art in which, at 33, she is already a veteran." Barney Josephson wanted Williams to act more like Scott, but she refused to do so. As it had with Katherine Dunham and Pearl Primus, the press often made comparisons between Scott and Williams, noting the former's coy sexiness and the latter's artistic seriousness. However, unlike the two dancers, Scott and Williams were devoted friends. When Scott left Café Society Uptown to marry Adam Clayton Powell Jr., Josephson replaced her with Williams.

For Williams, Hazel Scott was a beloved younger sister. Scott, in turn, adored Williams and referred to her as a "Saint." Scott had access to greater opportunity than Williams did and was the more famous of the two, but she would later fall upon hard times. In 1950, Scott became the star of the first television program hosted by a black woman. The fifteen-minute show first aired on July 3, 1950. But later that month her name appeared in the *Red Channels*, the notorious anti-Communist publication that led to the blacklisting of a number of entertainers.

Although Scott denied the charges, her show lost its sponsors; it was canceled in September. Scott's political problems were exacerbated by personal ones. In later years, after having separated from Powell, she moved to Paris. She recalled receiving checks and money orders from Williams, who may have been suffering her own financial difficulties. Williams was even maid of honor at Scott's second wedding. The two women loved and respected each other profoundly and had a lifelong friendship.[20]

At Café Society, Williams did three shows nightly, at 8:30 P.M., midnight, and 2:30 A.M. The 8:30 audience included parents and children. But as the evening grew late, the audience would change as well. Williams recalled: "Our 8:00 show was packed with dad, mother and smaller children. . . . After 8 females were not allowed without an escort. . . . It was really like being in a big family. . . . The clientele consisted of the elite yet even the poorest was welcome whenever they came to see their favorite artist."[21]

She described Café Society as a community, almost a family: "On Sunday nights we had a little party, just the staff and a few musicians. Hazel Scott, Thelma Carpenter, Billy Strayhorn, Aaron Bridges and Lena Horne and friends would come by and we'd have the most enjoyable time."[22] In between sets, Williams would sometimes sit with her close friend Gray Weingarten, a college student at Syracuse, in Weingarten's car. Sometimes she would join other musicians and the club's emcee, Johnnie Gary, at the backstage door for a game of cards and a smoke.

On any given night at Café Society one might have found the artist David Stone Martin sitting in the audience, listening to and looking at the brilliant, beautiful pianist. Martin wrote notes to Williams on postcards depicting the club's famous murals; sometimes he jotted down something on napkins as well. The two became very good friends; if his passionate letters to her are any indication, they became lovers as well. In her writings, Williams referred to him only as her good friend: "I met a very talented artist named David Stone Martin who today is very well known in the jazz world. I asked him to do an illustration cover for me for one of my albums. . . . We became quite chummy."[23] She may have been reluctant to acknowledge their romance because Stone was married at the time of their involvement. Williams helped to start Martin's career; he produced many fine line drawings for jazz album covers throughout the 1940s and 1950s. His aesthetic concept helped to shape the mood through which the music would be heard.

Whether they were friends or a couple, when they were together in public Williams and Martin were subjected to the same prejudice and attacks that other interracial couples had to endure. Williams sometimes met Martin at his Village studio, and they took long walks through the winding streets of that legendary neighborhood. Once they were harassed by a group of young white men who disapproved of them. The confrontation became violent, and though David tried to fend them off, the men seem to have gotten the better of him. In spite of its long history of political progressivism, the Village was not always welcoming to black people or to interracial couples.

Richard Wright's biographer Hazel Rowley noted that because there were several violent incidents in the Village, where Italian gangs assaulted interracial couples in the spring of 1944, Wright never allowed his wife to take his arm or hold his hand in the street. When Wright and his wife Ellen, who was of Polish Jewish descent, decided to buy a home in the Village, they had to have a white surrogate act in their behalf. The real-estate agents, banks, and neighbors would not have welcomed a black resident. They set up a corporation, "the Richelieu Company," to purchase the home.[24]

Martin also visited Williams in her Harlem apartment. There is no indication that they experienced similar harassment on the streets of Harlem. Ultimately, it seems, the inconveniences of Martin's marital status may have worn on the couple. Or perhaps Williams was able to maintain a relationship because he was married—and thus unable to really interfere with her artistic ambitions and her independent lifestyle. In any event, by 1945, the romantic relationship, if there was one, appears to have been over. Williams and Martin remained dear friends for life, but by the mid-forties, Williams was involved with another musician, Milton Orent.

Significantly, both Martin and Orent were white men. Williams had been married to only black men, and all of her romantic attachments before Martin had been to black men—all of whom were musicians. The love of her life was the great Ben Webster, a highly regarded jazz saxophonist, with whom she became involved in the thirties. Prior to moving to New York, her world had been primarily black. Although New York was segregated, her social life in the city was not. There, she found herself in the company of young, hip, progressive men and women of both races. This was her community. It centered on the music.

Williams began performing at Café Society Uptown in 1945. Located on East 58th Street, the larger club lacked the warmth and intimacy of the downtown venue. Williams preferred the downtown venue, noting that, "for all its looks, the Uptown Café was nothing like Downtown—though it catered for the same kind of Eastside crowd: movie stars, millionaires and the elite. Downtown was groovy, more relaxed than uptown."[25] Josephson felt Williams could be as big a star as Hazel Scott, however, and he believed the move uptown would expose her to a broader audience.

Following the move uptown, Josephson helped secure a weekly radio show for Williams on WNEW. Called *The Mary Lou Williams Piano Workshop*, the show gave her an extraordinary opportunity to reach listeners who did not come to Café Society. It also gave her the chance to try out new works before premiering them.

Some nights between shows, Williams went to 52nd Street, "the Street," to hear Billie Holiday at the 3 Deuces, or over to the Hurricane to see Duke Ellington's band. One night she sat in with the band when Duke was late. Fifty-second Street, between Fifth and Seventh Avenues, housed a number of clubs where on any given night you could hear stars from all eras of the short history of jazz: 3 Deuces, Kelly's Stable, the Hickory House, Leon & Eddies, Club Carousel, the Famous Door, the

Mary Lou Williams with fans in the studios of WNEW, the radio station that hosted *The Mary Lou Williams Piano Workshop*, 1945. Courtesy The Mary Lou Williams Collection, Institute for Jazz Studies, Rutgers University.

Onyx, Club Downbeat. Musicians, fans, and college students found their way to the Street, and so did the hustlers and the drug peddlers. Billie Holiday famously said, "I spent the rest of the war years on 52nd Street and a few other streets. I had the white gowns and the white shoes. And every night they'd bring me the white gardenias and the white junk." Williams never used heroin—nor did she drink; her substance of choice was marijuana. But she never passed judgment on those who became addicted. In fact, she later tried to set up a one-woman rehab in her apartment. She claimed, "It doesn't matter what a person does as long as I like him or he is blowing."[26] This was Mary's major criterion: first and foremost, she liked talented musicians who were disciplined and serious about the music.

On 52nd Street, Williams noticed the drug use, but she was there for the music. When she did comment about narcotics, it wasn't to spread tales about individual musicians, but to share observations about the ways unscrupulous people would plant drugs on unsuspecting musicians. At one of the clubs on 52nd Street, Williams was standing at the bar when a detective walked in. Another man, afraid of getting caught with whatever drugs he was carrying, hid them in a musician's coat that was lying on the bar. "A girl I happened to know took it out of his pocket without the musician, who was a nice guy and a nondrinker, [noticing what she'd done]," Williams later wrote. "She said to me, 'Did you see what that rotten so and so did? I guess he thought he'd be searched and rather than get in trouble he'd rather frame an innocent man.' After this I was told to keep my hands in my pockets if I had pockets whenever I was on the street."[27]

When Williams finally headed home, or in the afternoon before heading downtown, she might stop off to see Thelonious Monk and "the kids," as she called the young bebop musicians. Bebop was a harmonically complex, fast-paced style of music requiring near virtuosic skill. While swing bands allowed individual soloists to break away and improvise before returning to the arrangement, in bebop most of the tune was taken up by long, improvised solos over difficult chord changes. The music developed in small clubs; in after-hours jam sessions;

in some of the most innovative big bands, such as Billy Eck-stine's; and in the salonlike atmosphere of Williams's Hamilton Terrace apartment.

After Williams finished her work at Café Society, the young musicians would pick her up and head uptown to her apart-ment around 4 A.M. Miles Davis, Monk, Mel Tormé, Sarah Vaughan, Tadd Dameron, Bud Powell, and Dizzy Gillespie all found their way to 63 Hamilton Terrace: "Usually when Monk composed a song he'd play both night and day if you didn't stop him," Williams later wrote. "Bud, Monk or Tad would run to the house . . . playing their new things for my approval or showing them to me."[28] She became especially close to the young, gifted Bud Powell, encouraging Barney Josephson to hire him and then mentoring him both profes-sionally and musically.

But their creative relationship was mutual. Williams in-sisted, "The things Bud wrote for me improved what little orig-inality I had and inspired me to experiment with my own things." Williams is being unduly modest here. As early as 1940, especially on the album *Six Men and a Girl*, one can hear her using harmonies that would be associated with bop. She had referred to them as "weird harmonies" and "screwy chords." Williams was much more than a mentor, midwife, or maternal figure for the new music and the younger musicians; indeed, she was an active participant in and contributor to the techni-cal development of the music. In many ways she was both a pioneer, laying the groundwork and pointing out future direc-tions, and a student of bebop. She was always open to learning, changing, and growing, and thus she was constantly evolving as an artist.[29]

Like a number of other musicians, Powell fell in love with Williams. "Once or twice," she wrote, "I had to hide away because I think he felt he was in love with me—he wouldn't allow me even to sit with one of my little nephews. He wanted nobody around me. If I walked down the street with anybody he'd push them away from me. He began to depend on me emotionally." Eventually she had to distance herself from him because of his insane jealousy, further exacerbated by his mental illness and substance abuse. "I wouldn't let Bud Powell in my house when he'd come in high," Williams later said.[30]

For many of the men, Williams was more of a maternal figure than a paramour, and they treated her with tenderness and respect. What she thought of them and their music mattered to them. Later on, the brilliant and innovative Herbie Nichols wrote her pages and pages apologizing for not living up to her standards; he expressed remorse for his own drug use and for letting her down. The tone of the letter suggests that he may have been more devastated than she was over his failings because he so badly wanted to earn her approval.

Williams spent many predawn hours at Minton's on 118th Street to hear and support the "boppists." She wrote, "The cats fell into Minton's from everywhere, the customer had no place to sit for the instrument cases. I used to hear Mr. Minton grumble in a kidding way about all musicians packing the place and there wasn't much space left for the customers."[31] A throng of musicians, hipsters, students, and others who appreciated the music filled Minton's. Young white musicians came hoping to learn this exciting and innovative form that was being perfected among young black musicians. The beboppers created a counterculture as well as a music. Of course, many musicians of Williams's generation had no time or ear for the music that would become known as bebop, but Williams heard their originality and brilliance and continued to support, encourage, and teach them. She also recognized that many of those who dismissed the new music, both black and white, were not beyond stealing and incorporating their ideas without crediting the boppers.

By now, Williams found herself growing tired of all the benefit performances required of her as a Café Society musician. She told British jazz critic Max Jones, "The only drag in New York was the many benefit shows we were expected to do—late shows which prevented me from running up on 52nd Street to see my favorite modernists."[32]

In 1943, Williams began conceptualizing what would become one of her most significant and ambitious compositions, *The Zodiac Suite*. Ever since Duke Ellington had presented *Black Brown & Beige* at Carnegie Hall in January 1943, Williams had aspired to write an extended work of her own. She had recently begun to see Milton Orent, a classically trained bassist and arranger, and she and Orent worked together to prepare for the composition. They listened to live music. They went to the New York Public Library's branch on East 58th Street to listen to classical recordings, and they read the scores of Paul Hin-

demith, Arnold Schoenberg, Igor Stravinsky, and other German modernists and French Impressionists. Williams's friend
Gray Weingarten also brought music to her, and the two would
listen to and discuss them in Williams's apartment. According
to Weingarten, she introduced Williams to her favorites, the
Russian modernists, and in exchange Williams introduced
Weingarten to bebop. Still, Williams continued to think "bop
[was] the only real modern jazz, despite the contentions of
the copyists of Stravinsky, Hindemith and Schoenberg." During the period of composition, Williams attributed much of
her growth and development to her growing relationship with
Orent. Her friends disagreed. Weingarten feels that Williams
gave Orent credit because he was her boyfriend. Whatever the
case, the two spent a lot of time together, and he worked
closely with her on the extended composition and would eventually conduct it.[33]

At any rate, Williams was intent on diligently preparing herself for the production of her first extended work. She then began working on the suite at Café Society Uptown, composing
the first three movements and improvising them nightly. She
also introduced one *Zodiac* composition a week on her radio
show. Ultimately, Williams dedicated all twelve signs to her
artist friends and others involved in the music business. The
dedications are a virtual who's who of the New York jazz scene
at the time, with Ben Webster, Billie Holiday, Art Tatum, and
others on the list. Each piece evokes that individual's traits as
well as the dominant traits of the sign of the zodiac he or she
was chosen to represent.

Williams had a long-standing interest in the zodiac. At this stage in her life she hungered for spiritual meaning and guidance, but she did not have a sense of religiosity. For her, music was a spiritual medium, a conduit to something outside of herself as well as a vehicle for expressing a sense of the spiritual, if not the divine. She operated in a secular world, that of jazz and show business, yet the jazz world itself was nonetheless characterized by its own expressions of the spirit. Surprisingly, Williams found community in the context of New York nightlife, a world in which sex, drugs, and money were in great supply. But the scene also provided fellowship, warmth, love, and transcendence. She would later write: "Jazz is a spiritual music. It's the suffering that gives jazz its spiritual dimension."[34] For Williams, black music offered transcendence by directly confronting and acknowledging human suffering. This was the source of its spiritual power, for suffering and our longing for transcendence from it are what join us as humans. She believed black music to be a gift to all humankind because it provided a way through pain and suffering to beauty and joy.

Listening to the *Zodiac Suite* today, in these post–*Kinda Blue* times, one may be reminded of Miles Davis's seminal work. "Cancer," especially, sounds like the introduction to "So What." "Cancer" is deeply interior and moody, introspective and dark, but in a soothing, comforting way. It is impressionistic—but classical and modern at the same time. It leaps ahead a decade, previewing the sounds that would dominate the late fifties.

Pianist and educator Billy Taylor praised the suite's "innovative use of the rhythm section." Later, Andrew Homzy, writing a set of liner notes for the Vintage Jazz Classics edition of *Zodiac Suite*, called it "a series of vividly evocative tone poems in the jazz idiom." The piece is indeed poetic, at times haunting, at other times meditative. Here it is dancelike, there humorous. As with the twelve signs of the zodiac, each movement evokes a different mood and persona. Williams herself was a Taurus. That piece starts off as a quiet and introspective piano solo moved by a series of chords and two-note motifs before the drums join in, seeming to push the melody further over a series of repeated chords. Midway through, the left hand brings in a blues tone before the song returns to the meditative feel of the opening. "Taurus" melds directly into "Gemini," whose opening choruses echo the sound and energy of Broadway, or perhaps a Stuart Davis painting.

The larger work provided Williams the space to explore classical music and to attempt to bring together classical and jazz idioms. Williams wrote that *Zodiac* was "the beginning of a real fulfillment of one of my ambitions. As a composer and a musician I have worked all my life to write and develop music that was both original and creative." Although she found classical musicians—the paper guys—too studied and lacking in the creativity that characterized jazz musicians, she envisioned a group that would bring together black and white, male and female, European classical music and jazz—a truly democratic ensemble.

Williams debuted *The Zodiac Suite* with Edmond Hall's chamber orchestra at Town Hall at 123 West 43rd Street on a Sunday afternoon, New Year's Eve, December 31, 1945. The orchestra included a string section, a flute, a clarinet, a bassoon, and a number of brass instruments. Bassist Al Hall, drummer I. C. Heard, and an unknown opera singer joined the orchestra. Williams's friend and former lover Ben Webster was featured as well, as were Edmond Hall (clarinet), Henderson Chambers (trombone), and Eddie Barefield (tenor and clarinet). Milt Orent directed the orchestra. At the same concert, Williams also performed some of her most popular jazz and boogie-woogie tunes. The reviewer for the *New York Times* found the work "rather ambitious" and noted, "The composition was scarcely a jazz piece at all, making its appeal as a more serious work. How successfully, time will tell." Clearly, Williams had used the opportunity to expand her own vision beyond the parameters of what was conventionally called jazz, though it is highly unlikely she would have made the kinds of distinctions suggested by the reviewer.[35]

Jazz was still rare in the city's concert halls. Benny Goodman had performed the first concert by a jazz orchestra in Carnegie Hall in 1938, and Williams performed *The Zodiac Suite* there in 1946. Though founded by the League for Political Education as a meeting place to provide public education on important political issues, Town Hall quickly emerged as a preferred site for musical performances because of its incredible acoustics. Built by the architect firm McKim, Mead & White in 1919, Town Hall opened on January 12, 1921. It welcomed contralto Marian Anderson in 1935, and it was home to an extraordinary jazz concert on June 22, 1945, featuring Dizzy Gillespie, Charlie Parker, Don Byas, Al Haig, Curley Russell, and Max Roach. It was one of the venues that was most welcoming to jazz performers.

Through Williams's music, places of architectural and acoustic wonder, the concert halls, were transformed into spaces where traditions met, conversed, and sometimes collided; they were spaces where paper men met improvisational genius. Places like Café Society and Williams's Sugar Hill apartment brought together integrated groups of musicians and integrated audiences that challenged convention and tradition. This urge to challenge traditional sounds, spaces, and communities was reflected in the broader desires of progressive artists and activists, especially in Harlem. They remade the city in their own image, and they imagined and sought to bring into being their own version of a beloved community.

The acetates of the Town Hall performance were stolen and not recovered until more than forty-five years later. Williams's friend Timmie Rosenkrantz would eventually release the recording of the Carnegie Hall performance in Europe, but the recording of the live performance of the *Zodiac Suite* would not be available for decades in the United States.[36]

Moses "Moe" Asch recorded and released the studio version of *Zodiac* in 1945. Shortly after arriving in New York, Williams began to record for Asch, and she continued to do so during her most productive periods. Williams always admired and respected Asch. She noted, "The poor guy never quite made it financially because he was too nice to musicians." Williams was grateful to Asch for a number of reasons: "He submitted my music to all the New York libraries, he paid me for recording musicians I had heard in Pittsburgh," she explained. "Sessions for Asch brought me more royalties than

I've had from any other record company, and gave me the free-dom to create."[37]

Even after recording it, Williams continued to recompose and revise *The Zodiac Suite*. In addition, other artists performed portions of it. Williams's fellow Café Society performer and friend Pearl Primus choreographed and performed parts of it, and would continue to do so throughout the decade. Talley Beatty and Katherine Dunham also choreographed dances to portions of *Zodiac*. Williams dedicated "Scorpio" to Dunham, Imogene Coca, and Ethel Waters, whom she called "my friends the sexpots." Gray Weingarten arranged for Williams to per-form parts of the suite in Syracuse at a benefit for the NAACP. Dizzy Gillespie recorded three movements in 1957, arranging them for big band.

Following the whirlwind surrounding *The Zodiac Suite*, Williams took a much-needed break. The rush of writing, the anxiety and excitement about the performance, the nightly gigs at Café Society, the benefits, and all the recording sessions had contributed to her emotional and physical exhaustion. She requested a leave from the club; Josephson agreed, gave her a beautiful watch as a token of his gratitude and admira-tion, and let her go. Ordinarily, she would have gone home to Pittsburgh; seen her nieces, nephews, and sisters; enjoyed homemade cooking; and maybe sat in with local musicians. Unable to muster the energy this time, she stayed in New York. More specifically, she stayed in Harlem. She'd been so busy, she hadn't really gotten to know her neighborhood; it had been a place to eat and sleep, meet with other musicians, and workshop her music. At most, she would go to Minton's on 118th Street. The newspapers claimed that 118th Street was the most dangerous street in the city because of the crime, but Williams hadn't found that to be true. The people who hung out there got to know her, loved her, and treated her with courtesy and respect. The food at Minton's was good—a man named Lindsay Steele used to cook wonderful meals and then come out and sing during intermission.

Because of these experiences, Williams greatly looked forward to knowing the neighborhood more intimately. Like most musicians, she was a night person. She walked the streets of Harlem after the sun went down, when good, hardworking people were at home with their families. Ever the generous one, always wanting to help, and believing she could save people's lives, she became an easy mark. "I must have gone all over Harlem in about 4 weeks from Lenox to 7th and 8th Avenues [and] from Hamilton Heights to 135th and below."[38]

Postwar Harlem was a transformed place. It lacked the optimism that had characterized it during the war, and the neighborhood never recovered from the riots. Rows of abandoned, boarded-up buildings invited criminal activity. As the defense industry began to shut down and men returned from the war, many people who had found work in the defense industry and other forms of manufacturing now found themselves without work. The garment factories that had lined East Harlem in earlier times had closed and moved outside the city, leaving in their wake high rates of unemployment. Gangs and heroin had begun to dominate street life.

Williams found Harlem at night both fascinating and frightening: fascinating *because* it was frightening. "I had never in my life been in such a terrible environment with people who roamed the streets looking for someone to devour. . . . It was fascinating watching one race of people live off of the other. I wondered why with all their shrewd brains, they never ventured downtown."[39] By different races, she meant those who preyed and those who were preyed upon. Malcolm Little, then serving time in federal prison in Massachusetts, would later concur. Only months before, he, too, had walked these same streets, and he had been part of that "race of people" who preyed upon others.

Like an anthropologist or sociologist, an observer but not an objective one, Williams walked. "The new experiences began to mean a great deal to me," she later wrote. "I considered myself a guinea pig in finding out answers to certain downtown gossip concerning Harlem. I had read several books on the subject and thought the authors ridiculous or biased. Yet I can say it can be quite a hell hole if one is weak enough to go for all that happens here." This was the Harlem of Ann Petry's novel *The Street* and her article "Harlem." For both Petry and Williams, Harlem had become a ghetto. Williams had an extensive library and informed herself through reading and observation. She had lost any romantic sense of Harlem and had become aware of its underside. At the same time, her world was expanding significantly beyond the small, close-knit circle of musicians who constituted her family.[40]

Without the protection of her musician brothers, and distancing herself from her girlfriends, Williams let her naive curiosity get the best of her. She had successfully avoided the substances that plagued her friends, yet another habit, just as expensive, if not more so, awaited her: gambling. On the road between sets and gigs, she had always enjoyed the occasional card game with other musicians as a way to pass the time. The soirees at 63 Hamilton Terrace often included an occasional game of poker or tonk, but she had never been involved in any serious game where the stakes were high.

That would change when, one night, an acquaintance took her to a card game in one of Harlem's after-hours spots. Williams lost $150, but she was having a ball. On her nightly strolls, she encountered the elite and the denizens of the night, all of whom were hooked on gambling. "I was introduced to the cream of the crop . . . nice teachers, apartment owners, house-wives who'd come to the game with $5.00, others who if they lost, would pull out $200–300 more. The first game I played there were more than 'a few doctors' as well." At the gambling table she met the full cross-section of Harlem. "I remember the first big game I went to I was a nervous wreck for days, af-ter hearing all the loud mouth jive and big talk. Everyone talk-ing at the same time. It took some time to get used to this." Williams, the sensitive artist, was both stimulated and over-whelmed by her surroundings.[41]

Harlem supplied her with plenty of opportunities to pursue her new interest. "My name was ringing all over Harlem as the poker chump," she later wrote. Although Williams lost more and more money, she justified it by telling herself that her oppo-nents needed the money more than she did, "to keep their rent going and other necessities." Soon her friends and her two half-brothers, Jerry and Howard (who were living with her following stints in the army), expressed concern and alarm. But she paid no heed to them, later saying, "I continued to stay up working nights and gambling, never getting any rest until I had a breakdown [and] went to a doctor."[42]

She kept playing; she kept losing. The more she lost, the more she withdrew from her savings account. She withdrew so regularly, in fact, that federal authorities thought she was being blackmailed. "I must have stopped counting at $7,000," she wrote.[43] Some games would last as long as four days nonstop. There was constant stimulation. She emerged from them into the rose-colored dawn, dazed, but thrilled nonetheless. She also became involved with a new man, Lindsay Steele from Minton's. Steele was the first of Williams's lovers who was not an artist; he was a numbers banker. He also seemed to have offered her some protection in her new environment, though he didn't help her stop gambling.

After weeks of roaming the streets, hitting the after-hours spots, and sitting in on card games the way she used to sit in with musicians, Williams came to a conclusion about the city. "New York is a town [where] if one takes a vacation or relaxes and tries to be normal and nice something happens. To explore New York means certain death. One has to be tough and on the alert."[44] Williams began to experience New York as a place that was unsafe and unwelcoming to those who lacked the toughness required by life in the city. Suddenly, the city she loved, the city that had been a source of inspiration, became a place of "certain death," both literal and spiritual.

And yet, she didn't retreat. She pulled back from the gambling, but unlike many of her friends and other members of the middle class, she refused to leave Harlem, and she continued to be observant of and sensitive to her surroundings. After the riots, many of the upper middle class left as surrounding neighborhoods opened up to them. St. Albans, Queens, became the preferred dwelling place of the jazz elite. A middle-class community located just a few miles from JFK Airport, it is now the center of Queens's African American community. Jazz musicians began to move to large homes, especially those located in the Addisleigh Park neighborhood. Lena, Pops, Duke, and even Lady Day moved there. Williams's beloved Dizzy found his way to the outer borough. Count Basie moved there in 1946, and shortly afterward, Ella followed. Langston Hughes, Ralph Ellison, and Williams wouldn't leave. Even during its lowest points, Harlem maintained a middle-class presence, and these three were part of it.

One day, a young boy who lived on Williams's floor was shot and killed in a gang war. Young boys between the ages of eight and fifteen were particularly vulnerable to gang membership and gang violence. In 1946, the nine-year-old Claude Brown, who would go on to write the memoir *Manchild in the Promised Land*, was recruited into a Harlem gang. On the other side of town, in Spanish Harlem, where a growing population of Puerto Rican immigrants and their children lived, nineteen-year-old Piri Thomas, who later became the author of *Down These Mean Streets*, also a memoir, was already a veteran of street battles. So prominent would gang life become that in

1948 *Life* magazine ran a photo essay about a young gang leader named Red Jackson. The photographer, Gordon Parks, followed Jackson for months, befriending him, gaining his trust, and photographing him in ways that showed both his toughness and his vulnerability. Through the *Life* story, people across America got a glimpse of the violence that black urban dwellers already knew by experience. It was during this period that a growing discourse on juvenile delinquents emerged.

After the death of her young neighbor, Williams decided to devote herself to doing something for young people and for her community—that is what Harlem had become for her. Its residents were "her people." At first her efforts were philanthropic. "I decided to help with the situation," she explained, "through getting donations from people to build playgrounds, recreation rooms, etc."

But as early as the spring of 1946, Williams expressed an interest in doing the work herself. She began to reach out to public schools, seeking to work with young people there. In a letter dated June 8, 1946, she wrote to a school principal, "Unfortunately until now I have been unable to accept these invitations[,] many of which came from the 'trouble areas' so understandably in need of guidance. . . . I've been most unhappy at not having the time[;] if your office would approve the plan and arrange a schedule, I should be very, very happy to do two concerts weekly from now until the end of the present semester, at no charge naturally." If her earlier involvement in political and civic activity occurred at the prompting of Barney Josephson, Teddy Wilson, or John Hammond, in 1946, especially after having witnessed the conditions of the black poor firsthand, Williams set out on her own campaign. She did not limit her efforts to Harlem. On June 17, she wrote to the principal of Arts High School in Newark, New Jersey, explaining, "Playing jazz concerts for school audiences is one of the projects closest to my heart and knowing of your interest too, I am taking your suggestions and support in encouraging the board of education to approve and sponsor these programs."[45]

As the seasons changed, Williams continued to be concerned about Harlem and to think of ways to help alleviate the suffering she saw there, but she also turned her attention to the racial situation on a national level. In spite of some courtroom gains, Jim Crow still ruled the day, especially in the South. Her friends Hazel Scott and Katherine Dunham made headlines by refusing to play before segregated audiences. Pearl Primus had gone to the South two years earlier to witness in person the degradation blacks experienced there, and the trip had transformed her art. Inspired, in part, by the political tenor of the times, Williams decided to directly challenge segregation: she came up with a plan to form a racially integrated all-female band that would present a concert in the city of her birth, Atlanta. It is surprising that she chose to form an all-female band, given that she considered them novelties—she had often resisted any efforts to characterize her as a "woman" player. Perhaps she was inspired by the success of great bands like the International Sweethearts of Rhythm. More likely, she didn't want to risk an interracial co-ed band. Women were less threatening to segregationists.

Williams wanted to plan the concert for 1947; however, as is to be expected, she met with a great deal of resistance. Such a show would have been illegal in Georgia. Williams certainly knew this, but she persisted. In September 1946 she began corresponding with the Georgia governor, Ellis Arnall. She also enlisted the support of prominent individuals, asking them to send letters and telegrams to the governor in support of her efforts. Writing from Hyde Park on September 12, Eleanor Roosevelt suggested that Williams get in touch with novelist Lillian Smith. "She knows Georgia, she is sympathetic and could give you better advice than I could," Roosevelt wrote.[46] Lillian Smith was the white southern author of the antilynching novel *Strange Fruit*. Williams wrote to Smith, and to Walter Winchell, Orson Welles, and others as well. Winchell, who by now was assisting J. Edgar Hoover in his efforts to bring down Barney Josephson—and who later would have a terrible run-in with Josephine Baker—nonetheless did write to Governor Arnall at Williams's request. (In 1951, Baker was refused service at the Stork Club because of her race. On her way out, she yelled at Winchell, a frequent patron and booster of the establishment, because he did not come to her defense. In turn, he began to accuse her, in print, of having both fascist and communist sympathies.) Boxer Joe Louis telegraphed Williams, writing, "I am sending a telegram to Governor Arnall at your request. I hope this meets with success."[47]

On September 23, Williams received the governor's reply. He wrote, "I do not desire to get involved in the controversy your request would precipitate." Not to be deterred, Williams persisted, writing to Bill Nunn, managing editor of the *Pitts-*

burgh Courier. On October 1, Nunn promised to "get on this thing immediately and do everything in my power to help you out." He contacted Benjamin Mays, the distinguished president of Morehouse College, who served as mentor and model to generations of Morehouse men, including Martin Luther King Jr. In a November 1946 letter, Mays wrote to Nunn explaining the tense racial situation and the delicate balance of race relations in Atlanta at the time (see Appendix B). According to Mays, "It would be virtually impossible and certainly unwise right now for us to plan in Atlanta the kind of program Miss Williams suggested."[48]

Nunn forwarded this reply to Williams, and she kept it in a file of correspondence regarding her efforts until her death more than thirty years later. Williams must have been disappointed that her efforts were met with such disapproval. Surely, the experience seemed to demonstrate the difference between the progressive interracial circles in which she traveled and the strict limitations of life in the South. Those limitations were evident in both the continued commitment to racial segregation on the part of southern whites and the careful strategy taken by well-respected blacks. Williams's approach is somewhat telling: she did not first contact southern black leaders and request their assistance in her plan. Instead, she went to northerners in positions of power and influence, perhaps recognizing that the southern black leadership would be less likely to act in such a direct manner.

In addition to these more organized efforts to use her art to address major social issues of the day—Jim Crow and the growing rate of "juvenile delinquency"—Williams continued her own individual efforts to alleviate suffering. Gray Weingarten recalls going with Williams on expeditions of mercy to care and cook for sick musicians. She would try to set up a rehab clinic in her own apartment, bringing strung-out musicians into her home to help them kick their habits. Convinced of the healing power of music, she played it for these addicts and encouraged them to play through their cravings. "Any body who was sick or broke or out of food, she would say 'Gray, you gotta come help me,'" Weingarten remembers. According to Weingarten, they visited one musician and did fourteen loads of laundry in an effort to clean and organize his space. "There was no dryer, so she sent me to get rope and we strung it throughout the apartment in order to hang the wet clothing."[49]

During this period, Williams was drawn to a variety of forms of divination practices, many of which could be found in Harlem. Some were pure scams, while others were linked to long-standing spiritual practices, such as Hoo Doo, Voo Doo, and Santeria. "Before she got religion we did all kinds of crazy things," noted Weingarten, including visiting fortunetellers. This constant seeking hints at Williams's longing for a sense of spiritual direction and purpose. She visited diviners to seek guidance and solace. She played and composed music as a way of expressing her spiritual striving and to heal those who listened. And she engaged in personal acts of caregiving and charity, as well as larger, more political efforts, as a way of bettering her fellow human beings and her nation.

Six months into her break from Café Society, and having lost or given away a substantial part of her savings, Williams started performing again. The jazz world was beginning to undergo significant changes. As bebop replaced swing, uptown venues that had catered to dancers began to close. The new modern jazz, whose birth Williams had witnessed and nurtured, began to be identified with young men. Because of her age and her gender, she was no longer seen as an innovator by those who booked the clubs. And so she hit the road, leaving New York more and more often for work.

Williams continued to record and began to take on more students. At times, Julliard students made their way uptown, but Williams was very picky about the classically trained musicians with whom she would work. She did continue to serve as friend and mentor to younger musicians, however, and she began to publish her thoughts on and theories about the role of modern music. In November 1947 she published a short but important essay entitled "Music and Progress" that appeared in the *Jazz Record*. She explained, "Once a composer or a musician stops being aware of what is going on around him his music also stops."

The essay, which appears to be advice to younger musicians, contains a seed of the pedagogical stance she would develop in later years: "If we are to make progress in modern music, or, if you prefer, jazz, we must be willing and able to open our minds to new ideas and developments. If we decide that a new trend is real music we must work with that new trend and develop it to its peak of perfection." This statement underscores Williams's own practice. She helped to develop swing, boogie-woogie, and bop. She embraced newer musical innovations as they developed. If those who ran the business side of the music no longer thought of her as an innovator, musicians knew otherwise. Duke Ellington famously noted: "Mary Lou Williams is perpetually contemporary."[50]

Bop had opened Williams up to new possibilities in her own music. Having innovated in and then grown tired of swing and boogie-woogie, she found a new creative space in the arena of bop. "The music was so beautiful it just gave you a sight of a new picture happening in jazz. It had such a beautiful feeling. It didn't take me very long to get on to it or create in my own way," she wrote.

As Williams began to write her thoughts down in a more systematic way, she fleshed out this notion of musical development as it applied to black American music, insisting upon a connection between the earliest and the most modern forms. She wanted to impart a sense of history and purpose to modern jazz; she was also concerned that black Americans, and black American musicians, in particular, were in danger of losing—or, worse still, throwing away—their musical heritage. Even in the essay, a narrative of progress, Williams was situating "jazz" in the context of "modern music" and placing it alongside other highly regarded art forms: "When it has reached this so-called 'peak,'" she wrote, "it is really only the beginning, for then we build the new ideas on top of the old. This is not only progress in music, for the same is true for all forms of art including painting, sculpture, architecture, and even the theater."

Williams ended the essay with an expansive and inviting notion of the music she performed. "Modern music," she wrote,
"is not only limited to small groups of musicians." She cited the
Carnegie Hall Concert of 1946, where the New York Pops
symphony orchestra played her music, as an example. She also
stated her commitment to playing in as many venues, such as
universities, as possible. One gets the sense that Williams,
while always convinced of the magnitude, value, and complexity of black music, finally saw herself as one of that music's mis-
sionaries, ushering it into the halls of respectability.

Still, ensuring jazz's permanence and protecting its legacy
proved to be an uphill battle. A recording ban—which prevented musicians from recording for eleven months starting in
January 1948—as well as the closing of clubs on 52nd Street,
amounted to a severe blow to the New York jazz scene. Many
of the clubs were turned into strip joints. *Time* magazine be-
moaned the change, writing, "Along New York's Swing Lande,
where nightclubs in sorry brownstones crowd each other like
bums on a breadline, an era was all but over. Swing was still
there, but it was more hips than horns. Barrelhouse had de-
clined. Burlesque was back."[51]

Unable to record and having difficulty finding work in the
city, Williams got a job providing arrangements for Benny
Goodman's orchestra and eventually replaced Teddy Wilson,
at his suggestion, when he left the band. However, the arrangement didn't last. Goodman could be difficult to work with, and
he remained a little hostile to the new music. Williams, who by
now was incorporating many bebop ideas into her writing,

bumped heads with him. They did, however, record a few sides before parting ways.

Williams would spend the remainder of the decade composing and recording her own music. She received a commission from the director of a choir in her hometown of Pittsburgh in 1948 and enthusiastically took up the offer. Pittsburgh provided a change of pace and scenery and helped to revitalize her. Williams would often spend time with family, and she also made time to write. One composition, "Elijah Under the Juniper Tree," set to the poetry of Ray Monty Carr, provided Williams with the opportunity to experiment in a number of directions. With "Elijah," she wrote for voice, a first for her. The religious themes were new for her as well. With this piece she planted the seed that would flower years later in her Masses.

Back in New York, Williams's agent, Joe Glaser, continued to try to find bookings for her, but things were not working out. When Williams returned, she found that her beloved apartment had been burglarized, yet another indication of Harlem's desperation. Her records were gone, as were her gowns and her jewelry. In the words of writer Claude McKay, Sugar Hill had become "vinegar sour." Williams had become victim to the crime she had hoped to alleviate. Apart from a brief and successful stint at the Vanguard, Williams was unable to find work in the kinds of venues she wanted. Her surroundings had changed for the worse. In need of money and in poor health, Williams became despondent, exhausted, and depressed. In another blow, Moe Asch, her beloved record producer, went bankrupt in 1948.

Williams eventually signed with King Records, but it was not a good relationship. She wanted to record more experimental, bebop work as well as more solo work. King, in contrast, wanted commercial recordings. The company encouraged her to record swing music and do an organ album that would attract rhythm and blues audiences. Ultimately, the company refused to record her but would not release her from the contract. Williams sought the assistance of the American Federation of Musicians and was eventually released—but not without consequences: she always felt other recording companies saw her as a troublemaker.

Finally, Williams signed on with Circle Records, with whom she recorded solos as well as several of her bebop compositions and her experiments with bongos. The latter albums were released, but the solo material, which was to have been released as *Midnight at Mary Lou's*, would not appear until 2006, over fifty-five years after it had originally been recorded. Thanks to the tireless efforts of Father Peter O'Brien, a Jesuit priest and director of the Mary Lou Williams Foundation, all of the Circle material, including the solo medleys, is now available as *Mary Lou Williams: The Circle Recordings*. The work anticipates the solo concert Williams performed at the Montreux Jazz Festival in Switzerland in 1978. Here, in 1951, we hear the artist at her best—and her most personal. It is like listening to a sonic autobiography. The choice of material, the phrasing, and the chords all create a rich, deep, soulful listening experience. Lacking in pretense or sentimentality, the performance is intimate, but also an extraordinary display of Williams's genius at the instrument. The artist at forty, a woman who had already made major contributions to American music, here plays her history with an eye on the future. "Why," written by Consuela Lee, aunt of filmmaker Spike Lee, is especially beautiful. What's more, the performance also contains a history of black music, and as such is a sonic interpretation of American history. The music of the enslaved—the spirituals—branches out and is influenced by and influences American popular music. The medley starts with bars of music inspired by African American spirituals before turning to George Gershwin's "It Ain't Necessarily So," from the opera *Porgy and Bess*, which was itself inspired by black folk music. Then Williams turns to standards, recognizable popular songs over which jazz improvisers composed their own unique solos. All of these elements become vehicles for Williams's own improvisation, her personal history of jazz. The medley evolves into a music that captures the particular history of an individual, allowing her room for creativity and individual expression, yet it is also a music that contains the tragic and hopeful history of a people and a nation.

In these solos, Williams is a mature artist, capable of swinging but also of playing deeply introspective music. One can hear her Harlem stride background as well as her bop present, her strong left hand and each individual finger of the right hand as she caresses the keys. There is no doubt that she is in command of her genius and her instrument. She was still without a lucrative recording deal with a major label. She was both tired and restless. But she was the consummate artist.

For some time, Glaser had been encouraging Williams to tour Europe. Now, as she found it more difficult to find work,

and was facing financial difficulties, the idea was becoming attractive. As early as 1947, Williams began to consider his idea.
Many of her good friends were there, especially in Paris. Jazz
singer Inez Cavanaugh was living there and seemed quite
happy, in spite of being unable to find black hair-care products.
Williams would pack care packages and send them overseas.
For these Cavanaugh was grateful, writing, "Make[s] a cullud
girl happy just to see a jar of Dixie Peach."

On November 28, 1952, Williams attended a bon voyage
celebration in her honor. The guests included jazz innovators
Oscar Pettiford and Erroll Gardner. The next day she set sail on
the *Queen Mary*, headed for Europe, where she planned to stay
nine days. As it turned out, she would not return to New York
for two years.

During her time in Europe, Williams suffered what some
call a nervous breakdown. It might also have been a spiritual
crisis, "a dark night of the soul." Finding solace in Catholicism,
Williams abandoned music temporarily, only to return to it at
the encouragement of her spiritual mentors. In the years that
followed, she devoted much of her life to addressing human
suffering, especially what she witnessed in Harlem, and to ex-
ploring the deeply spiritual dimensions of the music called
"jazz." To Williams, these two projects—one humanitarian and
the other aesthetic—were one.

EPILOGUE

New York beckoned, and they came. They gave it sound and substance, word and music, dance and meaning. In turn, it gave them inspiration, a community, and an audience. It contributed to each one's already strong sense of self. It gave them the world. At the end of their careers, all three were honored by the city and its institutions.

But there was something unique about the 1940s. Perhaps it was a combination of the times and the women. A woman in her twenties and thirties is usually a vessel for life—most often bearing and rearing children. But sometimes, the creativity, brilliance, and energy required of mothering are available for other areas of a woman's life, particularly for creative and intellectual women. Their imagination is fertile; their stamina and concentration strong. Petry, Primus, and Williams were certainly not the only creative women living in New York, or even in Harlem. The city was teeming with them, though few acquired the fame and stature of these three.

All three experienced high points of creativity and celebrity during the early part of the decade. By decade's end, their stars

188

Harlem Nocturne. Alice Neel. 1952. Courtesy of Estate of Alice Neel.

had faded a little as the venues and organizations that had supported them closed or were transformed. Cultural tastes changed. The neighborhood they loved fell on hard times, and the nation they hoped to shape was still flawed. Women who had filled factories and offices during the war were asked to return home. The end of the decade saw the emergence of the Cold War, McCarthyism, and the "urban renewal" that followed in the wake of the Housing Act of 1949. Each of these developments would alter the contexts in which these women lived.

Painter Alice Neel, another Harlem-based artist and a contemporary of Primus, Petry, and Williams, portrayed this sense of change, closure, and nightfall in a painting entitled *Harlem Nocturne* (1952). Two high-rise apartment buildings sit on a barren landscape. Enclosed by a metal link fence and parallel to a lone, leafless tree, the buildings could be any of the modern apartment buildings one finds in Manhattan, but they most resemble the high-rise housing projects that began to sprout in poor neighborhoods. The buildings look institutional. Obvious in their absence are people. Like the leaves on the trees, they are gone from the streets. Perhaps they are inside the brightly lit apartments, but we see no evidence of them in the windows. *Harlem Nocturne* is not only Harlem at night, but Harlem after slum clearance, blight removal, and urban renewal. Harlem after "an epoch's sun declines."[1] This is the Harlem about which Petry wrote in her last article on the area; it is the Harlem that Mary Lou Williams walked prior to her departure for Europe.

Fortunately, the story does not end here, or rather, the end marks another beginning. Harlem experienced many new births, progressive politics did not die, and politically engaged artists would continue to answer their calling. So, too, does the sun rise again on the brilliant women of *Harlem Nocturne*.

The 1950s found Pearl Primus engaged in a variety of activities, personal and professional. She married twice, first to Yael Woll and then to Percival Borde, her collaborator and soul mate. She also gave birth to a son, Onwin. In 1959, she received a master's degree in education from New York University, and that same year she was named director of a new performing arts center in Liberia. Although her passport had been revoked in 1952, it was eventually returned, and she spent much of her time traveling throughout Africa and Europe. At the behest of the Liberian government, she choreographed *Fanga*, which would become one of her best-known dances. In 1978, she earned her PhD in dance education from New York University, received the Dance Pioneer Award from the Alvin Ailey American Dance Theater, and incorporated her Pearl Primus Dance Language Institute. Shortly thereafter, she became a professor of ethnic studies, artist in residence, and the first chair of the Five College Dance Department, organized under the Five College Consortium among Mount Holyoke, Amherst, Hampshire, and Smith Colleges and the University of Massachusetts at Amherst. In 1988, the American Dance Festival restaged her choreography for *Black Tradition in American Modern Dance*, a program seeking to preserve black dance. In 1991, President George H. W. Bush honored her with the National Medal of the Arts. The following year, the Kennedy Center held a Pearl Primus 50th Anniversary Concert.

Dance was the vehicle through which Primus expressed her intellectual and political commitments. Africa became central to these commitments as well as to Primus's growing sense of spirituality. Her devotion to the history and cultures of the continent never wavered. At the time of her death in 1994, the *New York Times* reported, "Her belief that there was material for dance in the everyday lives of black people—and her strong personality and early success—had a profound influence on several generations of black choreographers and dancers, among them Donald McKayle and Alvin Ailey."[2] McKayle and Ailey are not the only heirs of Primus's legacy. It lives on in the work of Jawole Willa Jo Zollar and her company, Urban Bush Women, and in the work of Primus's niece, Andara Koumba Rahman-Ndiaye, and her company, Drumsong African Ballet Theater (ABT). These two women and their respective companies continue two distinct but related components of Primus's artistic, intellectual, and political project. Dancer, singer, drummer, choreographer, and teacher, Rahman-Ndiaye, working in collaboration with her husband, Obara Wali Rahman-Ndiaye, founder and director of Drumsong, continues the work of her aunt by presenting the dance, history, and culture of Senegambia. Her intergenerational company features dancers, drummers, and singers young and old, male and female. Together they constitute an African-centered, spiritually driven community devoted to honoring the cultures of Africa and the diaspora. Zollar has choreographed two beautiful pieces inspired by Primus's own choreography as well as her journals and interviews, "Walking with Pearl . . . Africa Diaries" and "Walking with Pearl . . . Southern Diaries." Zollar may be one of the most energetic and consistent of

Primus's artistic heirs. She has not only choreographed works inspired by Primus, but is also building upon some of her earlier social and political commitments.

After moving back to Old Saybrook, Ann Petry gave birth to a daughter, Elisabeth, in January 1949. She published two more novels after *The Street: A Country Place* in 1947, and *The Narrows* in 1953. *The Narrows* would be Petry's last novel, but she continued to publish short stories and children's books. For the most part she remained out of the public eye, though she continued to be a participating member of her community. She continued to have faith in the democratic process as she remained actively involved in her town's politics, serving on its Republican Town Committee and running for and winning a seat on the school board.

In the 1970s and 1980s, a bevy of young black women writers began to publish highly original works of fiction: Toni Morrison, Alice Walker, Ntozake Shange, Gloria Naylor, and others would help to change the face of American literature. When Naylor, author of *The Women of Brewster Place*, was asked about her influences, she named Petry foremost among them. Petry offered an alternative to Zora Neale Hurston's "evocations" of black folk culture and to Richard Wright's masculinist urbanism. Petry hated the constant comparisons between herself and Richard Wright, but that may have been one price of renewed recognition. When establishing or creating a tradition, critics must identify the ways that books and authors speak to each other.

When Deborah McDowell, an important black feminist critic, founded and began to edit the Black Women Writers series for Beacon Press, she selected *The Street* to be part of the series. Although academic critics were the primary reasons for the renewal of interest in Petry's work, Petry did not like academic criticism, believing it created a barrier between reader and text. She found most academic criticism "uninteresting." Nonetheless, throughout the 1980s and 1990s, she and her work received more and more attention from critics. In 1996, in recognition of the fiftieth anniversary of the publication of *The Street*, literary critic and biographer Arnold Rampersad hosted a reading at New York's Town Hall, where the acclaimed actress Alfre Woodard read selections from the novel. By the time of Petry's death in 1997, this novel was appearing on college syllabi, Petry's fiction had been republished in new editions, and she had received numerous honorary degrees. In 1992, Trinity College hosted a daylong symposium and celebration in her honor. In 1997, her *New York Times* obituary noted that Petry "took a single stretch of Harlem and brought it vividly and disturbingly to life in her acclaimed 1946 novel, 'The Street.'"[3]

Mary Lou Williams returned to New York and to Harlem in December 1954. She found a church home in Our Lady of Lourdes Roman Catholic Church on 142nd Street. Dizzy Gillespie introduced her to Father John Crowley, who encouraged her to return to music as a vehicle for prayer and healing, both for herself and for others. Father Anthony S. Woods and a young priest named Father Peter O'Brien also served as her spiritual mentors. O'Brien became her manager as well. Williams was baptized into the Catholic faith on May 7, 1957, by Father

Woods and confirmed the following June. She returned to performing, and she founded the Bel Canto Foundation, which helped jazz musicians with substance abuse problems by assisting with their rehabilitation. Williams also opened a number of thrift stores in Harlem and used the funds she collected to help musicians.

Though she was performing again, Williams found it more difficult to do so in nightclubs. In the 1960s, she began to compose music inspired by her new faith that was still rooted in a jazz aesthetic, including "Black Christ of the Andes" (1963), a hymn in honor of St. Martin de Porres, and "Mass for Peace," also known as "Mary Lou's Mass" (1964). When her old friend and employer Barney Josephson opened a restaurant, the Cookery, Mary Lou convinced him to install a piano and have her play. He rented a piano, and in 1970 Williams began her residency there. Musicians came, old fans showed up, and young hipsters and college students came, too. She played there on and off until 1978. In 1977, she appeared at Carnegie Hall with the avant-garde pianist Cecil Taylor. That same year, when she was hired by Duke University, she was among the first group of African American jazz artists to obtain academic positions at major American universities. Her final recording, "Solo Recital," recorded at the Montreux Jazz Festival in Switzerland in 1978, is a testament to her genius, her spiritual maturity, her soulfulness, and her virtuosity. She died of bladder cancer in Durham in 1981.

There are many examples of Mary Lou Williams's musical legacy. The example she set was of someone who was constantly in the process of learning, evolving, even as she remained grounded in the tradition that claimed her. Her music carried and contained both personal and collective histories, and it acted as a conduit to create a community and to put listeners in touch with aspects of the divine. Even for the secular among us, there is no question that there is something deeply spiritual in her music. It isn't ethereal or otherworldly. Instead, her music is rooted and grounded in the specific sonic histories of African American music, putting listeners in touch with something that is both deeply internal and larger than themselves.

Many artists continue to be influenced by her music. Women artists, in particular, have found inspiration in Williams's example: in her insistence on making art and on being taken seriously as a contributor to musical culture, her leadership, and her sacrifice of celebrity in favor of artistic integrity. Her musical inheritance has been nurtured in a number of settings. The Mary Lou Williams Collective, led by Geri Allen, an arm of the Mary Lou Williams Foundation, is one of the most exciting incarnations. The Collective is devoted to performing and recording Williams's music and has recorded and released, for example, *Zodiac Suite: Revisited*. The Collective does not replicate Williams's music exactly as she recorded it, however. Allen, herself a highly accomplished, world-renowned musician, composer, and arranger, brings her sensitivity, intellect, and own spiritual strivings to Williams's music and is often called upon to perform tributes to her as a solo artist. In addition, she played Williams in the Robert Altman film *Kansas City*.

Other artists have also devoted their time and attention to ensuring that Williams's music is familiar to contemporary artists. They often work without media attention on grant support. Some of them, such as pianist Bertha Hope and bassist Carline Ray, knew and were mentored by Williams. Another pianist, Amina Claudine Myers, who is also an organist, has a style that is deeply soulful with a strong left hand, and therefore shares much with Williams. Vibraphonist Cecilia Smith has arranged Williams's compositions in order to present them to newer audiences. In honor of the centenary anniversary of Williams's birth, the Lincoln Center Jazz Orchestra devoted two evenings to arrangements and compositions by Williams.

It is not surprising that many of the earliest efforts to recognize and honor Mary Lou Williams are to be found under the rubric of "Women and" or "Women in" Jazz. The music festivals, panels, and academic works that first focused on Williams tended to do so because they had too often ignored the work of women and the force of gender in the analyses and materials that they made available. At first these projects were marked by efforts to challenge the canon, to search for foremothers, to rewrite history, and to recognize the role that sexism played in these artists' lives and in the failure to give them their due in death. Ironically, Williams herself never cared to be classified as a "woman" jazz artist. She felt this kind of categorizing would greatly diminish her work and her impact.[4]

Pearl Primus, Ann Petry, and Mary Lou Williams continued to lead productive lives well into their seventies and eighties. Their commitment to their art, their passion for justice, and their concern for humanity were consistent throughout their

lives. Their courage and creativity continue to inspire. Fortunately, each left a body of work and personal archive for future
generations to study, learn from, and build upon.

Unlike so many women artists before them, they did not die
in obscurity or poverty. Their legacies have not been ignored or
forgotten. In the 1940s, each of them was committed to a vision of America, indeed of the world, as a place where all
people had access to opportunity and possibility. Each of them
exposed the limits of American democracy as it was practiced
during their time, and each devoted herself and her work to
building a movement for social change. At times, their sense of
our nation's possibility was severely limited by the continued
injustice they witnessed, but they all believed in the necessity
of fighting to build a better day, to bring the dawn to new generations. The progressive political atmosphere they inhabited
and helped to define set the foundation for and gave birth to a
younger generation that emerged in the 1960s. And while the
newer generation separated itself—the New from the Old
Left; the Black Power movement from the civil rights movement; second-wave feminism from both the Old Left and the
civil rights movement; black feminists from Black Power and
the white women's movement—they all reached back and created a place to recognize and celebrate these women.

ACKNOWLEDGMENTS

The idea for this book was born at the Schomburg Center for Research in Black Culture in 2001. Much of the manuscript was written at the Dorothy and Lewis B. Cullman Center for Writers and Scholars in 2006–2007. I am especially indebted to these two branches of the New York Public Library for inspiring and nurturing *Harlem Nocturne*. Howard Dodson, Diana Lachatanere, Steven G. Fullwood, Mary Yearwood, and Khalil Gibran Muhammad at the Schomburg, and Jean Strouse, Adriana Nova, and the wonderful staff of Cullman Center, all deserve a special thank-you.

I am forever indebted to my colleagues and students at Columbia University. Shawn Mendoza and Sharon Harris offered tremendous support throughout the process of research and writing. Conversations with Robin D. G. Kelley and the late Manning Marable greatly helped me conceptualize and focus the project in its earliest stages. Robert O'Meally, Brent Hayes Edwards, George Lewis, and John Swzed offered advice, shared research tips, and listened whenever I needed to talk. Marcellus Blount, Fredrick Harris, Kellie Jones, Alondra Nelson, Saidiya Hartman, Ann Douglass, James Shapiro, Steven Gregory, Aaron Johnson, and Jean Howard provided support and laughter throughout the entire process. Ann Douglass continues to be an intellectual idol. I am grateful for her model and for her friendship. Joanna Dees and Victoria Phillips Geduld, both of whom were graduate students at Columbia while I worked on *Harlem Nocturne*, were generous with their research. Their forthcoming critical dance histories are going to shape the way we think about modern dance.

All members of the Jazz Study Group constituted my major intellectual community. Maxine Gordon, Diedra Harris-Kelley, Jacqui Malone, C. Daniel Dawson, Sherrie Tucker, Guthrie Ramsey, Penny Von-Eschen, and Salim Washington generously offered of their time and their knowledge.

Bill Santin and Marilyn Pettit at the Columbia University Archives and Michael Ryan, Director of Columbia University's Rare Book and Manuscript Library, were especially helpful as I sought to reconstruct Pearl Primus's time at Columbia and searched for a number of rare photographs. The research for this book could not have been completed without the assistance of archivists at the following institutions: the Howard Gottlieb Archival Research Center at Boston University, the American Dance Festival Archives at Duke University, the Institute of Jazz Studies at Rutgers University, the Mary Lou Williams Foundation, and the New York Public Library for the Performing Arts.

I have been blessed with a bevy of talented, meticulous, and intelligent research assistants: Kadji Amin, Courtney Diamond, Tahirah Hendricks-Keene, Allison Hamilton, Leslie McCracken, Patricia Lespinasse, Nydia Swaby, and the intrepid Marsha Jean-Charles. Thank you all.

I was especially fortunate to have access to relatives of Williams, Primus, and Petry. Andara Primus-King, niece of Pearl Primus; Bobbie Ferguson, niece of Mary Lou Williams; Elisabeth Petry, daughter of Ann Petry; and Ginny Neel, daughter-in-law of Alice Neel, each made time to speak with me and answer my questions. Elisabeth Petry was especially patient with my numerous requests.

Father Peter O'Brien, Director of the Mary Lou Williams Foundation, taught me more about Mary Lou Williams and her contributions to American music than anyone else. His devotion to Williams's legacy is unparalleled and I am forever grateful to him for all of his assistance and generosity. Geri Allen helped me hear, understand, and better appreciate the complexity of Williams's compositions. Conversations with Cecilia Smith were also very helpful. Through two long telephone interviews, Gray Weingarten, a longtime, close friend of Mary Lou Williams, nourished me with stories about Mary Lou Williams.

The Black Women's Intellectual and Cultural History Collective (BWICH) allowed me to workshop portions of the manuscript and to talk about issues related to black women's intellectual history with a group of stellar scholars. Thadious Davis, Cheryl Wall, and Barbara Savage gave me extensive and helpful comments. Barbara Savage has gone above and beyond anything I could have expected. She read the entire manuscript, helped me think through thorny issues, and lent an ear, a shoulder to cry on, and a lot of love and laughter throughout every phase of this project. Her intelligence, her kindness, and her assistance are among my greatest blessings.

Daphne Brooks, Carla Kaplan, Salamishah Tillet, Jerry Watts, Cornel West, the late Richard Long, Louis Massiah, Carroll Smith-Rosenberg, Gerald Horne, and Tammy Kernodle have written books and articles or made documentary films that were of great importance to me as I wrote this book. Each of them also offered support, shared information, and helped me in my thinking about history, culture, and politics. I have learned a great deal from each of them, and my book has benefited greatly from the material they made available to me.

CT Powell, Henry Rock, Vera Wells, and Khalilah Boone each introduced me to people who knew Primus, Williams, or Petry. They held the keys that opened very important doors. Deb Willis deserves a special thank you.

My agent Loretta Barrett is a constant source of support and encouragement. Loretta introduced the project to Lara Heimert at Basic Books. Lara has been everything one could wish for in an editor: intelligent, sensitive, insightful, and patient. She worked closely with me through a number of drafts and I learned to trust her eye and her judgment. It has been an honor to work with her and everyone at Basic Books. I am so pleased *Harlem Nocturne* found a home there. Katy O'Donnell, Assistant Editor at Basic, gave all of her attention and a tremendous amount of time to the penultimate draft of the book. Katherine H. Streckfus is an ideal copy editor, and Rachel King deftly ushered the manuscript through its final stages with grace and ease. Melissa Runstrom has also been very attentive and committed to this project.

My beautiful mother, to whom this book is dedicated, has always read everything I have ever written. She continues to do so. As I wrote this book I thought often of stories that she has shared with me throughout the years. Her memories of World War II, of black soldiers, my father's time in the navy, and forties fashion, music, and dance helped to shape my sense of the sound, look, and setting of *Harlem Nocturne*. She and my "sister" Imani Perry are companions to my soul. Imani's published writings, our daily correspondence, and rare long walks shape my thinking every single day. I am grateful to her for reading portions of this manuscript and for offering advice whenever I requested it. Our friendship is a place where it is safe to be vulnerable and where I always feel understood. My grandniece Karen Phyliss Lindsay and cousin Ann Carson are wonderful inspirations to me.

This book took much longer to complete than I expected. During the course of research and writing, I experienced a few life-changing events. I lost my cherished aunt, Eartha Mordecai, and my beloved big sister, Myra Lindsay, both to lung cancer. Their deaths sent me reeling, but my memory of them, their impeccable style and strength, and their never-ending support and love continue to sustain me. Also, nieces Karen Lindsay and Molaika Motley were taken away from us much too soon. During this period I also met, fell in love with, and married Obery M. Hendricks Jr. His courage and brilliance inspire me on a daily basis. In addition to his love, Obery also gave me the gift of family: daughters Tahirah M. Hendricks-Keene and Serena Kumara Grant, granddaughters Mariame and Diata Canon, and sister and brother-in-law Linda Hendricks-Motley and Dennis Motley. What a blessing you all have been.

APPENDIX A

FBI Memo to Herbert Hoover

11/5/52

The statement made by Primus consists, in effect, of a denial of any Communist activities and furnishes no information about any associates. It is a rather clever denial of Communist membership (although membership and sympathy during a certain period were admitted) and acquaintances. Primus refused to furnish any information about associates with the arguments that she could not possibly furnish information about Communist membership on the part of an individual unless she was absolutely sure that individual was a communist, and she was not even sure she was a communist herself. . . . It is difficult to evaluate Primus' honesty.

Office Memorandum United States Government. By L. B. Nichols. Written to Mr. Tolson November 21, 1952. File Number 100–332915.

APPENDIX B

Benjamin Mays Letter

Dear Mr. Nunn:

I have been a little slow in answering your letter of Oct 6 relative to Miss Mary Lou Williams. I have been studying the situation here in Atlanta and I have now come to the conclusion that it would be virtually impossible and certainly unwise right now for us to plan in Atlanta the kind of program Miss Williams suggested. Things are pretty tense right here in Atlanta now and some of us are working very carefully and quietly to avert what could become a major racial conflict here. There is an organization by the name of the "Columbians" that are doing things worse than the Ku Klux Klan. Although things seem to be under control, any thing can happen at anytime. It may be that later such a program as Miss Williams proposes would be quite in order.

Benjamin E. Mays, president of Morehouse College, to Bill Nunn, managing editor of the Pittsburgh Courier, [November 6, 1946], copy sent to Mary Lou Williams, Mary Lou Williams Collection, MC 60, Series 6, Box 1, Folder 8, Institute of Jazz Studies Rutgers University, Newark, New Jersey.

I am returning Miss Williams' letter, which you may want to keep. I am also suggesting that you may send her a copy of my letter if you think it is necessary.

With kindest regards and best wishes, I am

Yours truly,

Benjamin E. Mays
President

APPENDIX C

Selected Short Stories and Novels by Ann Petry

YEAR:	1943
TITLE:	"On Saturday the Siren Sounds at Noon"
PUBLICATION:	*The Crisis* (Dec.)
PLOT:	Children of main character burn in fire in small apartment.
INSPIRATION:	Newspaper story Petry covered for "my paper"
YEAR:	1944
TITLE:	"Doby's Gone"
PUBLICATION:	*Phylon* (Fourth Quarter, 1944)
PLOT:	Girl attends all-white New England school with imaginary friend, who disappears after she beats up her tormentors.
INSPIRATION:	Autobiographical
YEAR:	1945
TITLE:	"Like a Winding Sheet"
PUBLICATION:	*The Crisis* (Nov.)
PLOT:	Domestic abuse and spousal murder follow racial incident at work.
YEAR:	1946
TITLE:	*The Street*
PUBLICATION:	Houghton Mifflin
PLOT:	Single black mother Lutie Johnson struggles to raise her son in Harlem.
INSPIRATION:	Newspaper story about superintendent who taught boy to steal letters

(continues)

(continued)

YEAR:	1947	
TITLE:	"The Bones of Louella Brown"	
PUBLICATION:	*Opportunity* (Oct.–Dec.)	
PLOT:	The bones of a laundress are mixed up with the bones of a countess. Where will they be buried?	
YEAR:	1947	
TITLE:	"In Darkness and Confusion"	
PUBLICATION:	*Cross Section*	
PLOT:	Man's son, a soldier, is executed in Georgia, and he takes part in Harlem Race Riot of 1943.	
INSPIRATION:	Harlem Race Riot of 1943; *Amsterdam News* story about executed soldier in Georgia	
YEAR:	1947	
TITLE:	"Solo on the Drums"	
PUBLICATION:	*'47: The Magazine of the Year* (Oct.)	
PLOT:	Love gone wrong inspires jazz drum solo.	
YEAR:	1947	
TITLE:	*Country Place*	
PUBLICATION:	Houghton Mifflin	
PLOT:	Storm in New England town leads to melodrama.	
INSPIRATION:	Hurricane of 1938	
YEAR:	1953	
TITLE:	*The Narrows*	
PUBLICATION:	Houghton Mifflin	
PLOT:	Interracial romance leads to murder in a small New England town.	

SOURCES AND
SUGGESTED READING

Archival Sources

Ann Petry

The Ann Petry Collection, Howard Gotlieb Archival Research Center, Boston University

Ann Petry Portrait Collection, Schomburg Center for Research in Black Culture, New York Public Library

The James E. Jackson and Esther Cooper Jackson Papers, Elmer Holmes Bobst Library, New York University

The Tamiment Library and Robert F. Wagner Labor Archives, New York University

Pearl Primus

The Pearl Primus Collection, Duke University Libraries

The Pearl Primus Collection, Schomburg Center for Research in Black Culture, New York Public Library

Mary Lou Williams

The Mary Lou Williams Collection, Institute for Jazz Studies, Rutgers University

Mary Lou Williams Portrait Collection, Schomburg Center for Research in Black Culture, New York Public Library

Performing Arts Research Collections, Performing Arts Library at Lincoln Center, New York Public Library

Other Sources and Suggested Reading

Adams, George R. "Riot as Ritual: Ann Petry's 'In Darkness and Confusion.'" *Negro American Literature Forum* 6, no. 2 (1972): 54–60.

Allara, Pamela. *Pictures of People: Alice Neel's American Portrait Gallery*. Waltham, MA: Brandeis University Press, 1998.

Aschenbrenner, Joyce. *Katherine Dunham: Dancing a Life*. Champaign: University of Illinois Press, 2002.

Bambara, Toni Cade, and Eleanor W. Traylor. *The Black Woman: An Anthology*. New York: Washington Square Press, 2005.

Barber, Beverly Anne Hillsman. *Pearl Primus, in Search of Her Roots: 1943–1970*. PhD diss., Florida State University, 1984.

Biondi, Martha. *To Stand and Fight: The Struggle for Civil Rights in Postwar New York City*. Cambridge: Harvard University Press, 2006.

Brailey, Muriel Wright. *Necessary Knocking: The Short Fiction of Ann Petry*. PhD diss., Miami University, 1996.

Brandt, Nat. *Harlem at War: The Black Experience in WWII*. Syracuse: Syracuse University Press, 1996.

Carby, Hazel V. *Reconstructing Womanhood: The Emergence of the Afro-American Woman Novelist*. New York: Oxford University Press, 1989.

Certeau, Michel de. *The Practice of Everyday Life*. Translated by Steven F. Rendell. Berkeley: University of California Press, 2002.

Clark, Veve A., and Sara E. Johnson. *Kaiso! Writings By and About Katherine Dunham*. Madison: University of Wisconsin Press, 2005.

Cruse, Harold. *The Crisis of the Negro Intellectual: A Historical Analysis of the Failure of Black Leadership*. New York: New York Review of Books Classics, 2005.

Dahl, Linda. *Morning Glory: A Biography of Mary Lou Williams*. Berkeley: University of California Press, 2001.

DeFrantz, Thomas F. *Dancing Many Drums: Excavations in African American Dance*. Madison: University of Wisconsin Press, 2001.

Diehl, Lorraine B. *Over Here! New York City During World War II*. New York: HarperCollins, 2010.

DuBois, W. E. B. "Close Ranks." *The Crisis* 16, no. 3 (1918).

———. "Returning Soldiers." *The Crisis* 18 (1919).

Ervin, Hazel Arnett. *Ann Petry: A Bio-Bibliography*. New York: G. K. Hall, 1993.

Estrada, Ric, and Sigrid Estrada. "3 Leading Negro Artists, and How They Feel About Dance in the Community: 1. Eleo Pomare. 2. Arthur Mitchell. 3. Pearl Primus." *Dance* 42, no. 11 (1968).

Evans, Stephanie Y. *Black Women in the Ivory Tower, 1850–1954: An Intellectual History*. Gainesville: University Press of Florida, 2008.

Fledderus, France. *The Function of Oral Tradition in Mary Lou's Mass by Mary Lou Williams*. Master's thesis, University of North Texas, 1996.

Foulkes, Julia L. *Modern Bodies: Dance and American Modernism from Martha Graham to Alvin Ailey*. Chapel Hill: University of North Carolina Press, 2002.

Fullilove, Mindy. *Root Shock: How Tearing Up City Neighborhoods Hurts America, and What We Can Do About It*. New York: One World Books Trade / Ballantine, 2005.

Glaude, Eddie S. *In a Shade of Blue: Pragmatism and the Politics of Black America*. Chicago: University of Chicago Press, 2007.

Glover, Jean Ruth. *Pearl Primus: Cross-Cultural Pioneer of American Dance*. Ann Arbor: University of Michigan Press, 1989.

Gore, Dayo. *Radicalism at the Crossroads: African American Women Activists in the Cold War*. New York: New York University Press, 2011.

Gottschild, Brenda Dixon. *The Black Dancing Body: A Geography from Coon to Cool*. New York: Palgrave Macmillan, 2005.

Graff, Ellen. *Stepping Left: Dance and Politics in New York City, 1928–1942*. Durham, NC: Duke University Press, 1997.

Gregory, Steven. *Black Corona: Race and the Politics of Place in an Urban Community*. Princeton: Princeton University Press, 1999.

Guy-Sheftall, Beverly. *Words of Fire: An Anthology of African-American Feminist Thought*. New York: New Press, 1995.

Harvey, David. *The Urban Experience*. Baltimore: Johns Hopkins University Press, 1989.

Haygood, Wil. *King of the Cats: The Life and Times of Adam Clayton Powell, Jr.* Boston: Houghton Mifflin, 1993.

——. *Sweet Thunder: The Life and Times of Sugar Ray Robinson*. New York: Knopf, 2009.

Hendricks, Obery. *The Politics of Jesus: Rediscovering the True Revolutionary Nature of Jesus' Teachings and How They Have Been Corrupted*. New York: Doubleday, 2006.

Hoban, Phoebe. *Alice Neel: The Art of Not Sitting Pretty*. New York: St. Martin's Press, 2010.

Holladay, Hilary. *Ann Petry*. New York: Twayne, 1996.

Honey, Maureen. *Bitter Fruit: African American Women in World War II*. Columbia: University of Missouri Press, 1999.

Horne, Gerald. *Black Liberation / Red Scare: Ben Davis and the Communist Party*. Newark: University of Delaware Press, 1994.

——. *Race Woman: The Lives of Shirley Graham Du Bois*. New York: New York University Press, 2002.

Johnson, James Weldon. *Black Manhattan*. Cambridge: Da Capo Press, 1991.

Jones, Jacqueline. *Labor of Love, Labor of Sorrow: Black Women, Work, and the Family, from Slavery to the Present*, 2nd ed. New York: Basic Books, 2009.

Josephson, Barney, and Terry Trilling-Josephson. *Cafe Society: The Wrong Place for the Right People*. Champaign: University of Illinois Press, 2009.

Kelley, Robin. *Thelonious Monk: The Life and Times of an American Original*. New York: Free Press, 2009.

Kelley, Robin D. G. *Hammer and Hoe: Alabama Communists During the Great Depression*. Chapel Hill: University of North Carolina Press, 1990.

———. *Race Rebels: Culture, Politics, and the Black Working Class*. New York: Free Press, 1996.

Kernodle, Tammy L. *Anything You Are Shows Up in Your Music: Mary Lou Williams and the Sanctification of Jazz*. PhD diss., Ohio State University, 1997.

———. *Soul on Soul: The Life and Music of Mary Lou Williams*. Boston: Northeastern University Press, 2004.

Kraut, Anthea. *Choreographing the Folk: The Dance Stagings of Zora Neale Hurston*. Minneapolis: University of Minnesota Press, 2008.

Kufrin, Joan. *Uncommon Women: Gwendolyn Brooks, Sarah Caldwell, Julie Harris, Mary McCarthy, Alice Neel, Roberta Peters, Maria Tallchief, Mary Lou Williams, Eugenia Zukerman*. Piscataway, NJ: New Century, 1981.

Lieberman, Robbie, and Clarence Yang. *Anticommunism and the African American Freedom Movement: Another Side of the Story*. New York: Palgrave Macmillan, 2009.

Lipsitz, George. *Rainbow at Midnight: Labor and Culture in the 1940s*. Champaign: University of Illinois Press, 1994.

Litwack, Leon F. *How Free Is Free? The Long Death of Jim Crow*. Cambridge: Harvard University Press, 2009.

Lloyd, Margaret. *The Borzoi Book of Modern Dance*. Whitefish, MT: Kessinger, 2007.

Lubin, Alex. *Revising the Blueprint: Ann Petry and the Literary Left*. Jackson: University Press of Mississippi, 2007.

Mallozzi, Vincent M. "Behind the Lens, Continuing a Legacy." *New York Times*, January 11, 2010, www.nytimes.com/2010/01/11/nyregion/11photog.html?emc=eta1.

Manning, Susan. *Modern Dance, Negro Dance: Race in Motion*. Minneapolis: University of Minnesota Press, 2004.

Mary Lou Williams Trio. *Roll 'Em: The World Jam Session, 1944—Complete*. Solo Art, 1999.

McKay, Claude. *Harlem: Negro Metropolis*. New York: Harcourt, Brace, Jovanovich, 1968.

McKayle, Donald. *Transcending Boundaries: My Dancing Life*. New York: Routledge, 2002.

Morgan, Stacy I. *Rethinking Social Realism: African American Art and Literature, 1950–1953*. Athens: University of Georgia Press, 2004.

Mullen, Bill V. *Popular Fronts: Chicago and African-American Cultural Politics, 1935–46*. Champaign: University of Illinois Press, 1999.

Mullen, Bill V., and James Smethurst, eds. *Left of the Color Line: Race, Radicalism, and Twentieth-Century Literature of the United States*. Chapel Hill: University of North Carolina Press, 2003.

Neel, Alice, Ann Tempkin, Susan Rosenberg, and Richard Flood. *Alice Neel*. Philadelphia: Philadelphia Museum of Art, 2000.

Neel, Alice, and Amy Young. *Alice Neel: Black and White*. New York: Robert Miller Gallery, 2002.

Osofsky, Gilbert. *Harlem: The Making of a Ghetto: Negro New York, 1890–1930*. Lanham, MD: Ivan R. Dee, 1996.

Ottley, Roi. *New World A-Coming*. New York: Arno Press, 1968.

Pearl Primus and Her Company. New York: Paul Lovett, 1950.

Perpener, John. *African-American Concert Dance: The Harlem Renaissance and Beyond*. Champaign: University of Illinois Press, 2001.

Petry, Ann. *Miss Muriel and Other Stories*. New York: Dafina, 2008.

———. *The Street: A Novel*. Boston: Houghton Mifflin, 1998.

Petry, Elisabeth. *At Home Inside: A Daughter's Tribute to Ann Petry*. Jackson: University Press of Mississippi, 2008.

Prevots, Naima. *Dance for Export: Cultural Diplomacy and the Cold War*. Middletown, CT: Wesleyan, 1999.

Ramsey, Guthrie P., Jr. *Race Music: Black Cultures from Bebop to Hip-Hop*. Berkeley: University of California Press, 2003.

Ransby, Barbara. *Ella Baker and the Black Freedom Movement: A Radical Democratic Vision*. Chapel Hill: University of North Carolina Press, 2005.

Rorty, Richard. *Achieving Our Country: Leftist Thought in Twentieth-Century America*. Cambridge: Harvard University Press, 1998.

Rosen, Bernice. *New Dance Group: Movement for a Change*. London: Routledge, 2000.

Schwartz, Peggy, and Murray Schwartz. *The Dance Claimed Me: A Biography of Pearl Primus*. New Haven, CT: Yale University Press, 2011.

Scott, William B., and Peter M. Rutkoff. *New York Modern: The Arts and the City*. Baltimore: Johns Hopkins University Press, 1999.

Smith, Morgan, and Marvin Smith. *Harlem: The Vision of Morgan and Marvin Smith*. Lexington: University Press of Kentucky, 1998.

Sorell, Walter. *The Dance Has Many Faces*. Chicago: Chicago Review Press, 1992.

Stearns, Marshall, and Jean Stearns. *Jazz Dance: The Story of American Vernacular Dance*. New York: Da Capo Press, 1994.

Stowe, David W. "The Politics of Cafe Society." *Journal of American History* 84, no. 4 (1998): 1384–1406.

Theoharis, Jeanne, and Komozi Woodard. *Freedom North: Black Freedom Struggles Outside the South, 1940–1980*. New York: Palgrave Macmillan, 2003.

———. *Want to Start a Revolution? Radical Women in the Black Freedom Struggle*. New York: New York University Press, 2009.

Tuan, Yi-Fu. *Space and Place: The Perspective of Experience*. Minneapolis: University of Minnesota Press, 2001.

Tucker, Sherrie. *Swing Shift: "All-Girl" Bands of the 1940s*. Durham, NC: Duke University Press, 2000.

Wald, Alan M. *Trinity of Passion: The Literary Left and the Antifascist Crusade*. Chapel Hill: University of North Carolina Press, 2007.

Wall, Cheryl A. *Women of the Harlem Renaissance*. Bloomington: Indiana University Press, 1995.

Welsh-Asante, Kariamu. *African Dance: An Artistic, Historical and Philosophical Inquiry*. Trenton, NJ: Africa World Press, 1996.

Wenig, Adele R. *Pearl Primus: An Annotated Bibliography of Sources from 1943 to 1975*. Oakland, CA: Wenadance Unlimited, 1983.

West, Cornel. *Democracy Matters: Winning the Fight Against Imperialism*. New York: Penguin, 2005.

White, Deborah Gray. *Telling Histories: Black Women Historians in the Ivory Tower*. Chapel Hill: University of North Carolina Press, 2008.

Williams, Mary Lou, Al Louis, and Jack Parker. *The Zodiac Suite*. Washington, DC: Smithsonian Folkways, 1995.

Wilson, Mark K., and Ann Petry. "A MELUS Interview: Ann Petry. The New England Connection." *Melus* 15, no. 2 (1988): 71–84.

Wren, Elsa. Unpublished interview with Pearl Primus, 1982. Pearl Primus Collection, Duke University.

Wright, Patricia. *The Prime of Miss Pearl Primus*. Amherst, MA: Contact, 1985.

X, Malcolm, and Alex Haley. *The Autobiography of Malcolm X*. London: Penguin, 2001.

Zipp, Samuel. *Manhattan Projects: The Rise and Fall of Urban Renewal in Cold War New York*. New York: Oxford University Press, 2010.

NOTES

Prologue

1. Walt Whitman, "Manahattan," in *Leaves of Grass* (New York: 1867).

2. Ann Petry, "Harlem," *Holiday*, April 1949, 84.

Introduction

1. Martha Biondi, *To Stand and Fight: The Struggle for Civil Rights in Postwar New York City* (Cambridge: Harvard University Press, 2006), 6.

2. Richard Rorty, *Achieving Our Country: Leftist Thought in Twentieth Century America* (Cambridge: Harvard University Press, 1998), 43.

3. Ibid., 3.

4. Rorty distinguished between agents and spectators in the following way: "In the early decades of [the twentieth century], when an intellectual stepped back from his or her country's history and looked at it through skeptical eyes, the chances were that he or she was about to propose a new political initiative." This is in opposition to those who possess a "spirit of detached spectatorship, and the inability to think of American citizenship as an opportunity for action." Rorty, *Achieving Our Country*, 9, 11. Rorty is not without his critics. For our purposes, one of the most astute has been Eddie Glaude. Glaude chastised Rorty for evading "the more fundamental challenge that Baldwin's writings present to anyone willing to engage them: that America must confront the fraudulent nature of its life, that its avowals of virtue shield it from honestly confronting the darkness within its own soul." For Glaude, too, much of the Reformist Left celebrated by Rorty failed to fully "work to diminish human suffering and make possible the conditions for human excellence," because of "their equivocation in the face of white supremacy's insidious claims." Eddie S. Glaude, *In a Shade of Blue: Pragmatism and the Politics of Black America* (Chicago: University of Chicago Press, 2007), 3.

5. Mary Helen Washington's description of the playwright Alice Childress also applies to Primus, in that she "concoct[ed] for herself, in true Popular Front fashion, a politics that was part Marxist, part black nationalist, part feminist, and part homegrown militancy." Mary Helen Washington, "Alice Childress, Lorraine

Hansberry, and Claudia Jones: Black Women Write the Popular Front," in *Left of the Color Line: Race, Radicalism, and Twentieth Century Literature of the United States*, Bill V. Mullen and James Smethurst, eds. (Chapel Hill: University of North Carolina Press, 2003), 185.

6. Biondi, *To Stand and Fight*, 13.

Chapter 1: Pearl Primus: Dancing Freedom

1. W. E. B. DuBois, "Close Ranks," *The Crisis* 16, no. 3 (1918): 111. See also W. E. B. Du Bois's editorial "Returning Soldiers," *The Crisis* 18 (1919): 13.

2. Karen Tucer Anderson, "Last Hired, First Fired: Black Women During World War II," *Journal of American History* 69, no. 1 (1982): 82–97. The Fair Employment Practices Committee became the Fair Employment Practices Commission in 1948, during the Truman administration.

3. Quoted in Wil Haygood, *King of the Cats: The Life and Times of Adam Clayton Powell, Jr.* (Boston: Houghton Mifflin, 1993), 93.

4. Pearl Primus, "African Dance," reprinted in *African Dance: An Artistic, Historical and Philosophical Inquiry*, Kariamu Welsh Asante, ed. (Trenton, NJ: Africa World Press, 1998), 3.

5. Langston Hughes, "On Leaping and Shouting," originally published in *Chicago Defender*, July 3, 1943; republished in *Langston Hughes and the Chicago Defender: Essays on Race, Politics, and Culture: 1942–1962*, Christopher C. Santis, ed. (Champaign: University of Illinois Press, 1995), 199.

6. John Martin, *The Modern Dance* (New York: Dance Horizons, 1966; originally published in 1933), 12.

7. See Evelyn Brooks Higginbotham, "The Metalanguage of Race," *Signs* 17, no. 2 (1992): 251–274.

8. Helen Fitzgerald, "A Glimpse of a Rising Young Star," *Daily Worker*, June 3, 1943, 7.

9. VeVe Clark and Sara E. Johnson, eds., *Kaiso! Writings By and About Katherine Dunham* (Madison: University of Wisconsin Press, 2005), 347. Little has been written about Pearl Primus, and that which has been written tends to focus on this period—her emergence in the 1940s or accounts of her as a grand dame of African dance on the American stage toward the end of her career. When writing about this period, most scholars rightly focus on her involvement with the New Dance Group and her dances of social protest. This is also my interest here; however, I hope to show her dance life during this period in a more fully dimensional way. Most often scholars writing of Primus's interest in Africa imply that her involvement in leftist politics preceded her first trip to Africa in 1948. I argue that it was her interest in Africa that preceded both her involvement in modern dance and her leftist politics.

10. See Robin D. G. Kelley, *Hammer and Hoe: Alabama Communists During the Great Depression* (Chapel Hill: University of North Carolina Press, 1990); Robin D. G. Kelley, *Race Rebels: Culture, Politics, and the Black Working Class* (New York: Free Press, 1996); Dayo F. Gore, *Radicalism at the Crossroads: African American Women Activists in the Cold War* (New York: New York University Press, 2011); Erik S. McDuffie, *Sojourning for Freedom: Black Women, American Communism, and the Making of Black Left Feminism* (Durham, NC: Duke University Press, 2011).

11. Beverly Anne Hillsman Barber, "Pearl Primus, in Search of Her Roots, 1943–1970" (PhD diss., Florida State University, 1984), 13.

12. Irma Watkins Owens, *Blood Relations: Caribbean Immigrants and the Harlem Community, 1900–1930* (Bloomington: Indiana University Press, 1996).

13. "Coming to the United States," n.d., Schomburg Center for Research in Black Culture, www.inmotionaame.org/migrations/topic.cfm?migration=10&topic=5.

14. Pearl Primus Journals, August 1937, Pearl Primus Collection, Duke University, Box 1, Journal Correspondence.

15. Ibid.

16. Ibid.

17. Barber, "Pearl Primus."

18. Lorraine B. Diehl, *Over Here! New York City During World War II* (New York: HarperCollins, 2010), 170; Maureen Honey, ed., *Bitter Fruit: African American Women in World War II* (Columbia: University of Missouri Press, 1999), 35. "Arsenal of democracy" is the phrase used by Franklin D. Roosevelt to describe the role of the United States in providing the United Kingdom with military supplies to help defeat Germany.

19. Barber, "Pearl Primus," 158.

20. Ibid., 117.

21. Richard C. Green, "Upstaging the Primitive: Pearl Primus" and "The Negro Problem in American Dance," in *Dancing Many Drums: Excavations in African American Dance*, Thomas F. DeFrantz, ed. (Madison: University of Wisconsin Press, 2001).

22. John Martin, "The Dance: Five Artists," *New York Times*, February 21, 1943.

23. John Martin, "The Dance Laurel Award No. 2," *New York Times*, August 1, 1943.

24. Susan Manning, *Modern Dance, Negro Dance: Race in Motion* (Minneapolis: University of Minnesota Press, 2004), 167. As Manning has noted, "for Martin, Dunham fulfilled the potential of Negro dance, while Primus merged themes that were racially authentic like Dunham's Negro dance, with themes that were individually expressive, like modern dance."

25. "Con Deleighbor, Katherine Dunham vs. Pearl Primus: Styles and Purposes in Negro Folk Dancing," *Amsterdam News*, February 12, 1944, 11A.

26. Interview conducted with Katherine Dunham, African American Music Collection, Haven Hall, University of Michigan, www.umich.edu/~afroammu/standifer/dunham.html.

27. David W. Stowe, "The Politics of Café Society," *Journal of American History* 84, no. 4 (1998): 1384–1406.

28. Unpublished interview with Elsa Wren, 1982, Pearl Primus Collection, Duke University, 5 ("Wren interview" hereafter); Barney Josephson and Terry Trilling-Josephson, *Cafe Society: The Wrong Place for the Right People* (Champaign: University of Illinois Press, 2009), 170–171.

29. Ibid.

30. Wren interview.

31. "Little Primitive," *Time*, August 25, 1947; "Genuine Africa," *Time*, May 21, 1951.

32. Peggy Schwartz and Murray Schwartz, *The Dance Claimed Me: A Biography of Pearl Primus* (New Haven, CT: Yale University Press, 2011), 31–33.

33. Susannah Walker, *Style and Status: Selling Beauty to African American Women, 1920–1975* (Lexington: University Press of Kentucky, 2007), 180; Phyl Garland, "The Natural Look: Many Negro Women Reject White Standards of Beauty," *Ebony*, June 1966, 143.

34. Wren interview, 5.

35. Barber, "Pearl Primus," 158.

36. "John Cage: Database of Works," n.d., John Cage Trust, http://www.johncage.org/pp/John-Cage-Works.cfm.

37. Lewis Allan was a penname; Allan's real name was Abel Meeropol.

38. "Pearl Primus: Artistic Summary," n.d., Dance Language Institute Archive, www.mamboso.net/primus/summary_3.html.

39. "Negro Women with White Husbands," *Jet*, February 21, 1952; see also *Jet*, February 14, 1952, 11. For the date of Primus's marriage to Borde, see Schwartz and Schwartz, *The Dance Claimed Me*, 269.

40. *Daily Worker*, September 28, 1944; quoted in Federal Bureau of Investigation (FBI) File No. 100–61887, September 1944, Report by William A. Costello, 22.

41. Margaret Lloyd, *The Borzoi Book of Modern Dance* (Whitefish, MT: Kessinger, 2007), 247.

42. Barber, "Pearl Primus," 106.

43. See Lloyd, *Borzoi Book of Modern Dance*.

44. Wren interview, 9.

45. Author interview with Esther Cooper Jackson, June 20, 2011.

46. Pamphlet, "National Integrity and Security Make Negro Youth of the South Assets of Democracy," James E. Jackson and Esther Cooper Jackson Papers, Elmer Holmes Bobst Library, New York University, Box 6, Folder 29 ("Jackson Papers" hereafter).

47. Kelley, *Hammer and Hoe*, 207; Jackson Papers, Correspondence, Pearl Primus to James Jackson, July 8, 1946, Box 14, Folder 5.

48. FBI File No. 100–61887.

49. Ibid.

50. FBI File No. 100–332915, May 30, 1945.

51. Lloyd, *Borzoi Book of Modern Dance*, 271.

52. Donald McKayle, *Transcending Boundaries: My Dancing Life* (New York: Routledge, 2002), 23.

53. Jawole Willa Jo Zollar, conversation with Peggy and Murray Schwartz, Schomburg Center for Research in Black Culture, May 24, 2012.

54. Barber, "Pearl Primus," 176–177. Barber describes Primus's technique in the following manner:

1. A distinctive carriage of the torso, use of the feet, and isolation of specific body parts
2. Forward lean of the body toward the earth
3. Forward inclination toward the earth
4. Feet contacting the floor fully to resemble caressing of the earth

55. Julia Foulkes, *Modern Bodies: Dance and American Modernism from Martha Graham to Alvin Ailey* (Chapel Hill: University of North Carolina Press, 2002), 70–71; Wren interview, 4.

56. Josephson and Trilling-Josephson, *Cafe Society*, 256–257.

57. Esther Cooper Jackson, who had been the subject of extensive FBI surveillance and investigation and had been very active in Communist Party circles, said that she never heard anything about Primus having been an informant. Author interview with Esther Cooper Jackson, June 20, 2011.

58. Sapphire, *The Kid* (New York: Penguin, 2011), 195.

Chapter 2: Ann Petry: Walking Harlem

1. The date of Petry's birth is listed differently in a number of publications, and Petry herself gave different dates for her birthday. Her official birth certificate says October 20, 1908. Throughout her career, she often gave the date October 12, but the years varied from 1908 to 1912. Family records indicate October 12, 1908. The town clerk of Old Saybrook once informed Petry that the doctor who signed her birth certificate dated a batch of certificates according to the date he submitted them.

2. Elisabeth Petry, *At Home Inside: A Daughter's Tribute to Ann Petry* (Jackson: University of Mississippi Press, 2008), 38.

3. Ibid.

4. Ibid., 38–39.

5. Ibid., 45.

6. Ibid., 43.

7. Petry journal entry, quoted in ibid., 166.

8. Petry, *At Home Inside*, 164.

9. E-mail correspondence with Elisabeth Petry, March 23, 2011; Elisabeth Petry, "What I've Finished Reading," http://lizr128.wordpress.com/2011/03/12/what-i%E2%80%99ve-finished-reading/. George Petry also recalled his experience in the DC church, speaking to the author in June 1993.

10. These descriptions come from photographs taken by Morgan and Marvin Smith. See James A. Miller, *Harlem: The Vision of Morgan and Marvin Smith* (Lexington: University Press of Kentucky, 1998).

11. Nat Brandt, *Harlem at War: The Black Experience in WWII* (New York: Syracuse University Press, 1996), 156; see also the survey of 1,008 blacks and 501 whites in New York, conducted in the spring of 1942 and published by the Extensive Surveys Division, Bureau of Intelligence, Office of Facts and Figures, as "The Negro Looks at the War: Attitudes of New York Negroes Toward Discrimination Against Negroes and a Comparison of Negro and Poor White Attitudes Toward War-Related Issues," Report 21, May 19, 1942. The Office of Facts and Figures became the Office of War Information.

12. Patrick S. Washburn, *A Question of Sedition: The Federal Government's Investigation of the Black Press During World War II* (New York: Oxford University Press, 1986), 178.

13. Not all American leftists abandoned the Communist Party, and among those who did, a number remained committed to leftist politics. Others adopted more liberal or conservative stances. For insightful discussions of American leftist intellectuals and writers and their reactions to the revelations about Stalin, see Alan Wald's two insightful studies, *Trinity of Passion: The Literary Left and the Antifascist Crusade*, and *American Night: The Literary Left in the Era of the Cold War*. Both were published by University of North Carolina Press, 2007 and 2012, respectively.

14. Wald, *Trinity of Passion*, 108–109.

15. Hazel Arnett Ervin, *Ann Petry: A Bio-Bibliography* (Boston: G. K. Hall, 1993), 9.

16. Ibid., xxiv.

17. Wald, *Trinity of Passion*, 119.

18. Nina Mjagkij, ed., *Organizing Black America: An Encyclopedia of African American Associations* (New York: Routledge, 2001).

19. Dayo F. Gore, *Radicalism at the Crossroads: African American Women Activists in the Cold War* (New York: New York University Press, 2011), 39.

20. "Ann Petry," in Adele Sarkissian, ed., *Contemporary Authors: Autobiography Series*, vol. 6 (Detroit: Gale, 1987). 253–269.

21. See African American Registry, http://www.aaregistry.org/historic _events/view/american-negro-theater-formed; see also Langston Hughes, Milton Meltzer, and L. Eric Lincoln, *A Pictorial History of Black Americans* (New York: Crown, 1956).

22. Ervin, *Ann Petry*, xiii.

23. "New York/Chicago: WPA and the Black Artist," Exhibition at the Studio Museum in Harlem, November 13 thru January 8, 1978, Essay by Ruth Ann Stewart, Guest Curator.

24. Ibid., xiv.

25. "Ann Petry," in Sarkissian, ed., *Contemporary Authors?*

26. Ibid.

27. Alain Locke, "Inventory at Mid-Century: The Literature of the Negro for 1950," Phylon 12, no. 2 (1951).

28. Bill V. Mullen, *Popular Fronts: Chicago and African-American Cultural Politics, 1935–1946* (Champaign: University of Illinois Press, 1999), 133.

29. See Appendix C.

30. Petry, *At Home Inside*, 95.

31. "Ann Petry," in Sarkissian, ed., *Contemporary Authors*, 265.

32. Ibid., 152–153.

33. Maureen Honey, *Bitter Fruit: African American Women in World War II* (Columbia: University of Missouri Press, 1999), 8.

34. Boots has a dangerous operation on his ear so that he is unable to pass the physical examination required by the military. Malcolm X appeared at the induction center dressed in his zoot suit and professed a desire to "organize them nigger soldiers . . . steal . . . some guns, and kill up crackers." Malcolm X, *Autobiography of Malcolm X* (New York: Grove Press, 1965). Dizzy Gillespie could have been reading from a script written by Petry when he told the army psychiatrist: "Well, look, at this time, in this stage of my life here in the United States whose foot has been in my ass? The white man's foot has been in my ass hole buried up to his knee in my ass hole! Now, you're speaking of the enemy. You're telling me the German is the enemy. At this point, I can never even remember having met a German. So if you put me out there with a gun in my hand and tell me to shoot at the enemy, I'm liable to create a case of 'mistaken identity', of who I might shoot." Dizzy Gillespie, with Al Fraser, *To Be, or Not . . . to Bop* (Minneapolis: University of Minnesota Press, 2009 [1979]), 120.

Both Malcolm X and Dizzy Gillespie were classified 4-F (registrant not acceptable for military service).

35. The full marketing plan is printed in Lawrence P. Jackson, *The Indignant Generation: A Narrative History of African American Writers and Critics, 1934–1960* (Princeton: Princeton University Press, 2011), 228–229; see also Hazel

Arnett Ervin and Hilary Holladay, *Ann Petry's Short Fiction: Critical Essays* (Westport, CT: Praeger Press, 2004), xviii.

36. Stacy I. Morgan, *Rethinking Social Realism: African American Art and Literature, 1930–1953* (Athens: University of Georgia Press, 2004), 2.

37. Ann Petry, "The Novel as Social Criticism," in *The Writer's Book*, Helen Hull, ed. (New York: Harper Brothers, 1950), 33.

38. Ibid.

39. Ibid.

40. For a brilliant discussion of Cootie Williams, see Guthrie P. Ramsey Jr., *Race Music: Black Music from Bebop to Hip-Hop* (Berkeley: University of California Press, 2003). Ramsey writes: "Williams's music provides a clear example of the stylistic flux in black popular music during the war years. In fact, I view this group as a progressive, early R&B band" (p. 69). As a band leader, Ramsey wrote, Williams "drew on many resources . . . : the repertory of his Ellington years, the jazz and swing tradition of his youth, the diverse talents of new instrumentalists and vocalists such as Powell, Vinson, and Davis, the innovations of new composers such as Monk, and the novel sounds of two emerging styles, bebop and rhythm and blues" (p. 72).

41. See Gerald Horne, *Black Liberation / Red Scare: Ben Davis and the Communist Party* (Newark: University of Delaware Press, 1994), 102. See also "Race Bias Denied as Rioting Factor: Spokesman for Negro Groups Lay Harlem Disorders to Sporadic Hoodlumism," *New York Times*, August 3, 1943.

42. "Ann Petry," in Sarkissian, ed., *Contemporary Authors*, 265.

43. On the young Malcolm X, the culture that produced him, and the relationship of that culture to the kind of proto-revolutionary consciousness that Malcolm Little, "Big Red," inhabits, see Robin D. G. Kelley, *Race Rebels: Culture, Politics, and the Black Working Class* (New York: Free Press, 1996).

44. Records of the Harlem Magistrate, August 1943, Municipal Archives, New York.

45. Lawrence P. Jackson, *The Indignant Generation: A Narrative History of African American Writers and Critics, 1934–1960* (Princeton: Princeton University Press, 2010), 145–146.

46. If Wright is a literary relative, so, too, is Marita Bonner. Bonner, a New Englander like Petry, graduated from Radcliffe; moved to DC, where she wrote essays and experimental plays; then married and moved to Chicago, where she began to master the short story. She created a fictional black neighborhood, "Frye Street," for her stories about Chicago's black migrants. Like Petry, Bonner published in *The Crisis and Opportunity,* but during the 1930s.

47. "Ann Petry," in Sarkissian, ed., *Contemporary Authors*, 265.

48. See Steven Gregory, *Black Corona: Race and the Politics of Place in an Urban Community* (Princeton: Princeton University Press, 1999), 27.

49. See Martha Biondi, *To Stand and Fight: The Struggle for Civil Rights in Postwar New York City* (Cambridge: Harvard University Press, 2003), 164.

50. Ann Petry, "Harlem," *Holiday*, April 1949, 84.

Chapter 3: Rollin' with Mary Lou Williams

1. Born September 8, 1903, in Dawson, Georgia, Davis went on to attend Morehouse and Amherst Colleges before enrolling at Harvard Law School. By the time he arrived in New England, he already had experienced protests against Jim Crow. On July 5, 1923, he was arrested in Atlanta because, like Petry's Sam, he refused to obey Jim Crow laws governing city buses.

2. Gerald Horne, *Black Liberation / Red Scare* (Newark: University of Delaware Press, 1994), 108; John C. Walter, *The Harlem Fox: J. Raymond Jones and Tammany, 1920-1970* (New York: State University of New York Press, 1989), 110; *Amsterdam News*, October 30, 1943, A8.

3. *New York Times*, November 14, 1943, 52.

4. Ann Petry, "Harlem," *Holiday*, April 1949, 84.

5. Mary Lou Williams, Autobiographical Notebook #2, 281, Mary Lou Williams Collection, MC 60, Series 5, Box 1, Folder 2, Institute of Jazz Studies, Rutgers University, Newark, New Jersey.

6. See Tammy Kernodle, *Soul on Soul: The Life and Music of Mary Lou Williams* (Boston: Northeastern University Press, 2004), 103.

7. Mary Lou Williams interview by John S. Wilson, June 26, 1973, transcript, p. 130, Jazz Oral History Project, Institute of Jazz Studies, Rutgers University, Newark, New Jersey ("Wilson interview" hereafter).

8. Wilson interview, 32.

9. Linda Dahl, *Morning Glory: A Biography of Mary Lou Williams* (New York: Pantheon, 2001); Kernodle, *Soul on Soul*.

10. Dahl, *Morning Glory*, 9.

11. Mary Lou Williams, "Jazz Is Our Heritage," Mary Lou Williams Collection, MC 60, Series 5, Box 2, Folder 38, Institute of Jazz Studies, Rutgers University, Newark, New Jersey.

12. Quoted in Dahl, *Morning Glory*, 11; Wilson interview, 4. See also Tera Hunter, *To 'Joy My Freedom: Southern Black Women's Lives and Labors After the Civil War* (Cambridge: Harvard University Press, 1998). Harlem stride was a highly percussive style of jazz piano developed in New York during the 1920s. Virtuoso improvisers, stride pianists were considered among the elite of New York's early jazz musicians. Stride pianists were also known for their "leaping left hands."

13. Kernodle, *Soul on Soul*, 13.

14. Telephone conversation between author and Bobbie Ferguson, July 2012.

15. Dan Morgenstern, ed., *Living with Jazz: A Reader* (New York: Random House, 2009).

16. Petry, "Harlem"; telephone conversation between author and Gray Weingarten, January 11, 2011.

17. Kernodle, *Soul on Soul*.

18. New York, March 7, 1944, originally on World Broadcasting Systems.

19. Williams, Autobiographical Notebook #2, 265–267.

20. See Karen Chilton, *Hazel Scott: The Pioneering Journey of a Jazz Pianist, from Café Society to Hollywood to HUAC* (Ann Arbor: University of Michigan Press, 2010).

21. Mary Lou Williams, Autobiographical Notebook #3, Mary Lou Williams Collection, MC 60, Series 5, Box 1, Folder 3, Institute of Jazz Studies, Rutgers University, Newark, New Jersey.

22. Max Jones, *Talking Jazz* (New York: Norton, 1988), 204.

23. Williams, Autobiographical Notebook #2, 290.

24. Hazel Rowley, *Richard Wright: The Life and Times* (New York: Henry Holt, 2001), 297, 350.

25. Jones, *Talking Jazz*, 205.

26. Williams, Autobiographical Notebook #2, 275.

27. Ibid., 275–276.

28. Ibid., 268–269.

29. See Dahl, *Morning Glory*, 115, 187.

30. Quoted in ibid., 188.

31. Williams, Autobiographical Notebook #2, 273.

32. Jones, *Talking Jazz*, 204.

33. Ibid., 204; telephone conversation between author and Gray Weingarten, January 11, 2011.

34. "Roots: The Little Piano Girl of East Liberty," n.d., Institute of Jazz Studies, Rutgers University, Newark, New Jersey, http://newarkwww.rutgers.edu/ijs/mlw/roots.html.

35. Though Williams often appeared in the *Amsterdam News*, the *Zodiac Suite* was not reviewed there. Barry Ulanov, writing for *Metronome* in February 1946, found the suite underrehearsed and sloppy in places. Nonetheless, he commended Williams for the courage of her musical convictions.

36. Rosenkrantz and his wife Inez Cavanaugh endeared themselves to many musicians. Gray Weingarten remembers parties at their apartment where Billie Holiday and Langston Hughes might be in attendance. She also remembers that Rosenkrantz encouraged the musicians to play and then recorded them without their knowledge. Many of these recordings were released in Denmark.

37. Jones, *Talking Jazz*, 202.

38. Williams, Autobiographical Notebook #3, 374.

39. Ibid., 376.

40. Ibid., 379–380; telephone conversation between author and Gray Weingarten, January 11, 2011.

41. Mary Lou Williams, Autobiographical Notebook #4, 432–433, Mary Lou Williams Collection, MC 60, Series 5, Box 1, Folder 4, Institute of Jazz Studies, Rutgers University, Newark, New Jersey; Williams, Autobiographical Notebook #3, 376.

42. Williams, Autobiographical Notebook #3, 375; Williams, Autobiographical Notebook #4, 434–435.

43. Williams, Autobiographical Notebook #3, 375.

44. Ibid., 378.

45. Mary Lou Williams to Mr. Roy Norris, June 17, 1946, Mary Lou Williams Collection, MC 60, Series 5, Box 4, Folder 1, Institute of Jazz Studies, Rutgers University, Newark, New Jersey.

46. Eleanor Roosevelt to Mary Lou Williams, September 12, 1946, Mary Lou Williams Collection, MC 60, Series 6, Box 1, Folder 8, Institute of Jazz Studies, Rutgers University, Newark, New Jersey.

47. Joe Louis to Mary Lou Williams, September 23, 1946, Mary Lou Williams Collection, MC 60, Series 6, Box 1, Folder 8, Institute of Jazz Studies, Rutgers University, Newark, New Jersey.

48. Governor Ellis Arnall to Mary Lou Williams, September 23, 1946, Mary Lou Williams Collection, MC 60, Series 6, Box 1, Folder 8, Institute of Jazz Studies, Rutgers University, Newark, New Jersey; Benjamin E. Mays to Bill Nunn, in copy sent from Bill Nunn to Mary Lou Williams, November 6, 1946, Mary Lou Williams Collection, MC 60, Series 6, Box 1, Folder 8, Institute of Jazz Studies, Rutgers University, Newark, New Jersey.

49. Telephone conversation between author and Gray Weingarten, January 11, 2011.

50. Duke Ellington, *Music Is My Mistress* (New York: DaCapo Press, 1976), 169.

51. "Manners and Morals," *Time*, March 8, 1948.

Epilogue

1. Jean Toomer, "Song of the Son," in *Cane* (New York: Boni and Liveright, 1923).

2. Jennifer Dunning, "Pearl Primus Is Dead at 74; A Pioneer of Modern Dance," *New York Times*, October 31, 1994.

3. Robert McG. Thomas Jr., "Ann Petry, 88, First to Write a Literary Portrait of Harlem," *New York Times*, April 30, 1997.

4. These contexts also paid special attention to the gendered dimension of the lives and works of women artists. In so doing, they challenged our very understandings of the cultural milieus these women inhabited and the vocabularies we use to discuss them.

INDEX

Abyssinian Baptist Church, 22, 91, 118

ACLU. *See* American Civil Liberties Union

Africa, 10, 24, 25, 31, 42, 54, 57, 72, 75

African Americans. *See* Black Americans

Ailey, Alvin, 68, 76, 191

Allan, Lewis, 53, 64, 66, 74

America. *See* United States

American Bar Association, 98

American Civil Liberties Union (ACLU), 75

American Dream, 89, 90, 108, 112

American Medical Association, 98

American Negro Theater (ANT), 101–103

American Nurses Association (ANA), 98–99

Ammons, Albert, 45

Ammons, Gene, 12

Amsterdam News, 23, 43, 85, 86, 92, 94, 118, 134, 137, 140

ANA. *See* American Nurses Association

Anderson, Marian, 48, 166

Angelou, Maya, 49, 131

Anna Lucasta, 102

ANT. *See* American Negro Theater (ANT)

Armed services. *See* Military

Art
for art's sake, 116
in Harlem, NY, 32
movement in, 16

politics and, 2–3, 12, 14
Popular Front and, 5
as propaganda, 116
social justice and, 30

Asch, Moses "Moe," 167–168, 182

Attaway, William, 114

Auden, W. H., 128

Autobiography (Franklin), 108

Bailey, Dixie, 150fig

Baker, Ella, 110

Baker, Harold, 14, 54, 147, 148

Baker, Josephine, 11–12, 176

Baldwin, James, 9, 13, 115–116, 117, 120, 127

Baltimore Afro-American, 140

Bambara, Toni Cade, 131

Bandy, Robert, 119, 124

Basie, Count, 136, 138, 139, 173

Bearden, Romare, 104

Bears-Bailey, Kim, 66–67

Beatty, Talley, 30, 31, 63, 168

Bebop. *See* Music

Belasco Theater, 63, 67

Benedict, Ruth, 71

Bennett, Gwendolyn, 104

Bethune, Mary McLeod, 37

Bible, 11, 116, 117

Black Americans
civil rights and, 5
class differences and, 27
Communist Party and, 20
confinement within mobility and, 17, 27
culture and, 3
dance and, 42